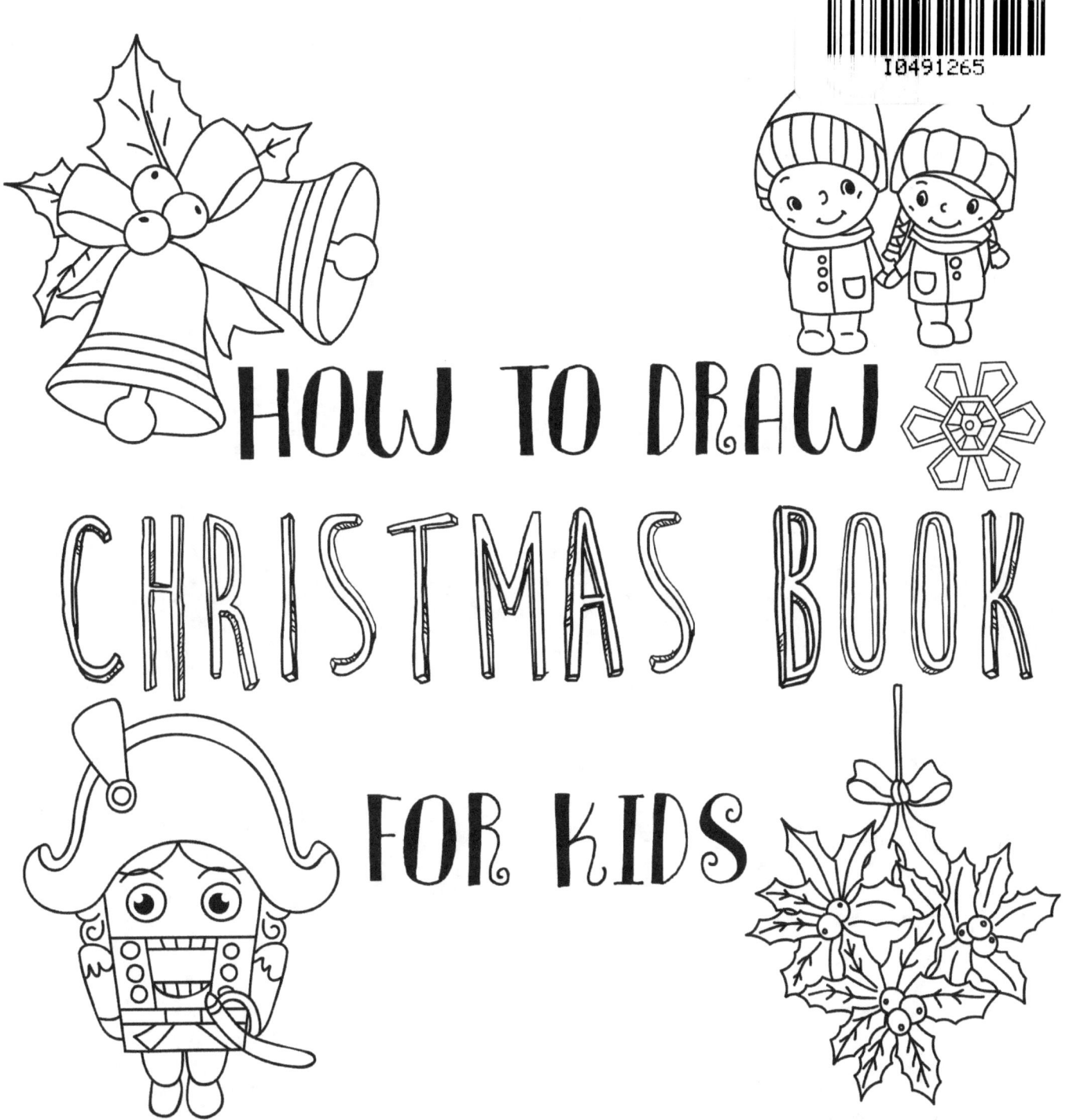

HOW TO DRAW CHRISTMAS BOOK FOR KIDS

THIS WONDERFUL BOOK BELONGS TO:

_____

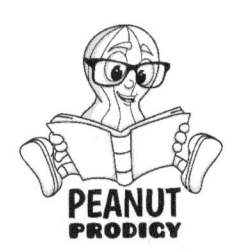

THINK YOU HAVE WHAT IT TAKES TO WIN OUR DRAWING CONTEST ?

We want you to draw your favorite picture from the book and send it into our Young Artists Drawing!

Please have your parents email us your illustration and we will select an entry to win our fully equipt art case every other month!

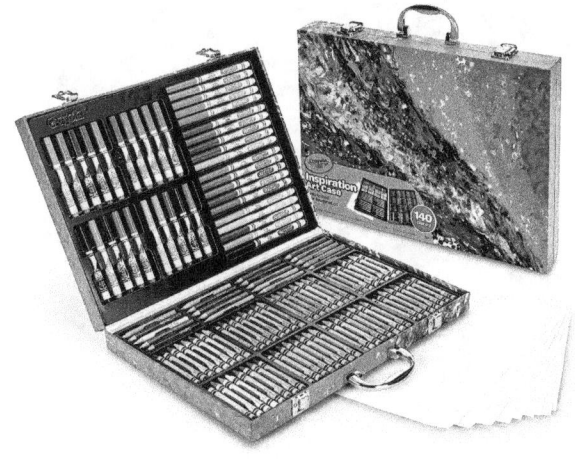

Email us your picture to:

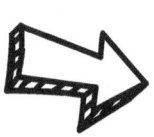 peanutprodigypublishing@gmail.com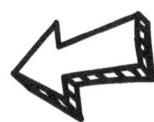

If you enjoyed this book as much as we do, please also leave us a review on Amazon. Your support is what keeps us going!

Happy Drawing!

-Peanut Prodigy Team

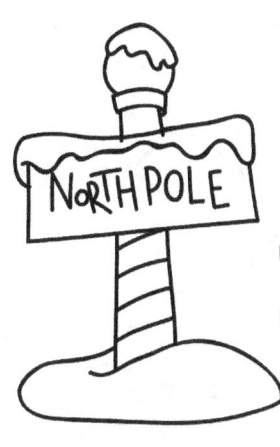

INSTRUCTIONS:

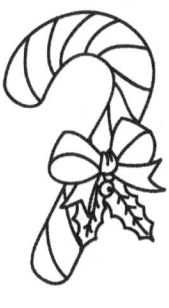

- Get ready to draw! Grab a pencil or a pen to get started.

- On the right side of the book, carefully imitate the drawings on the left side, step-by-step.

- Bring your picture to life with beautiful colors using markers, crayons, colored pencils, or watercolor paint!

- Keep your picture or give it to someone you love!

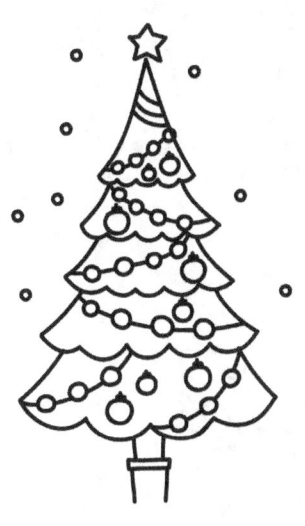

Merry Christmas!

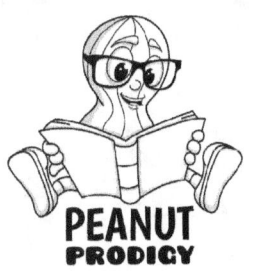

PEANUT
PRODIGY

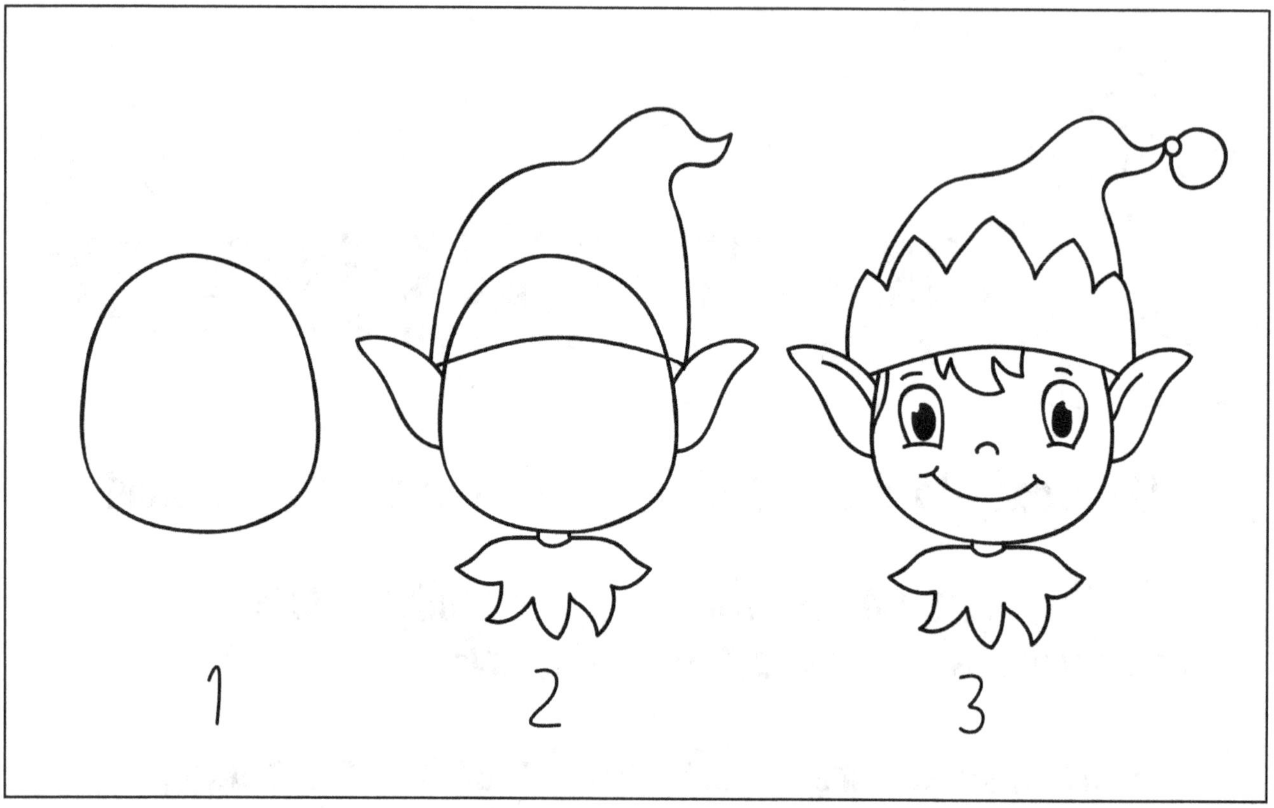

1

2

3

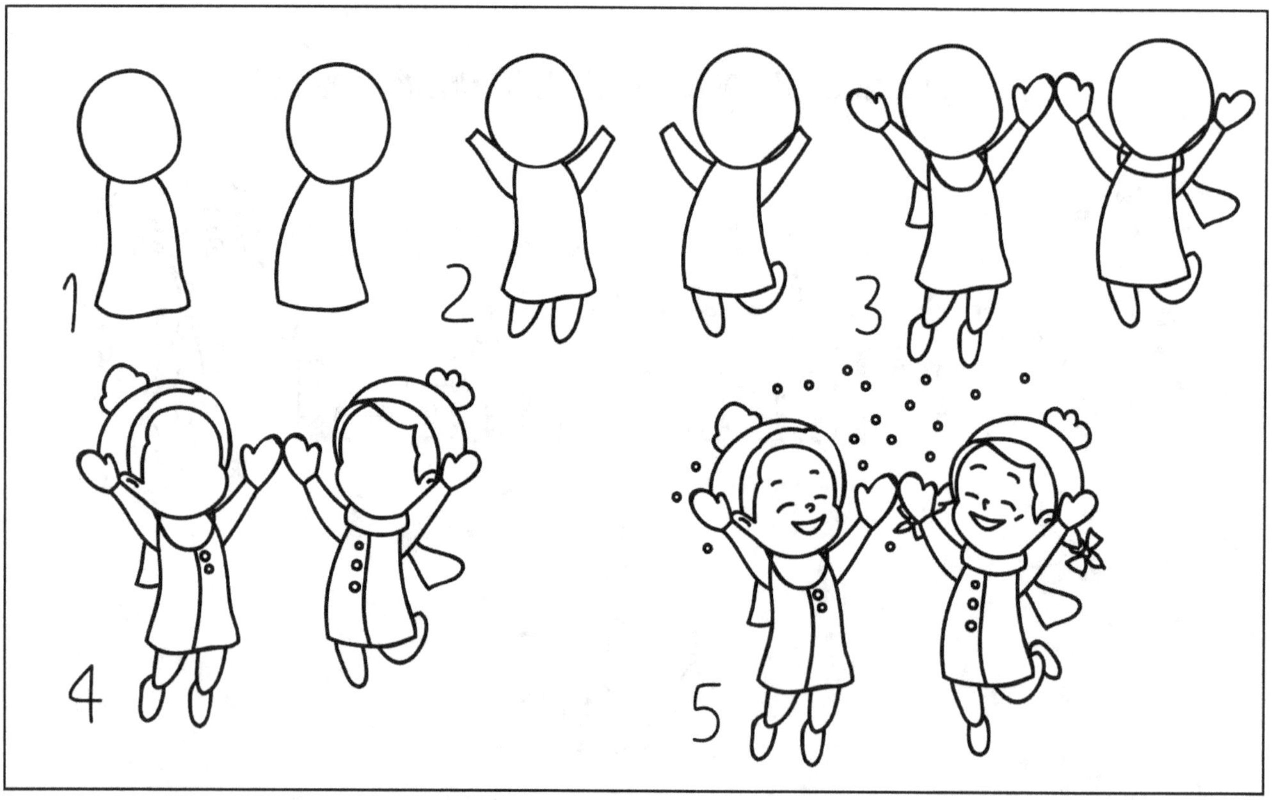

1

2

3

4

5

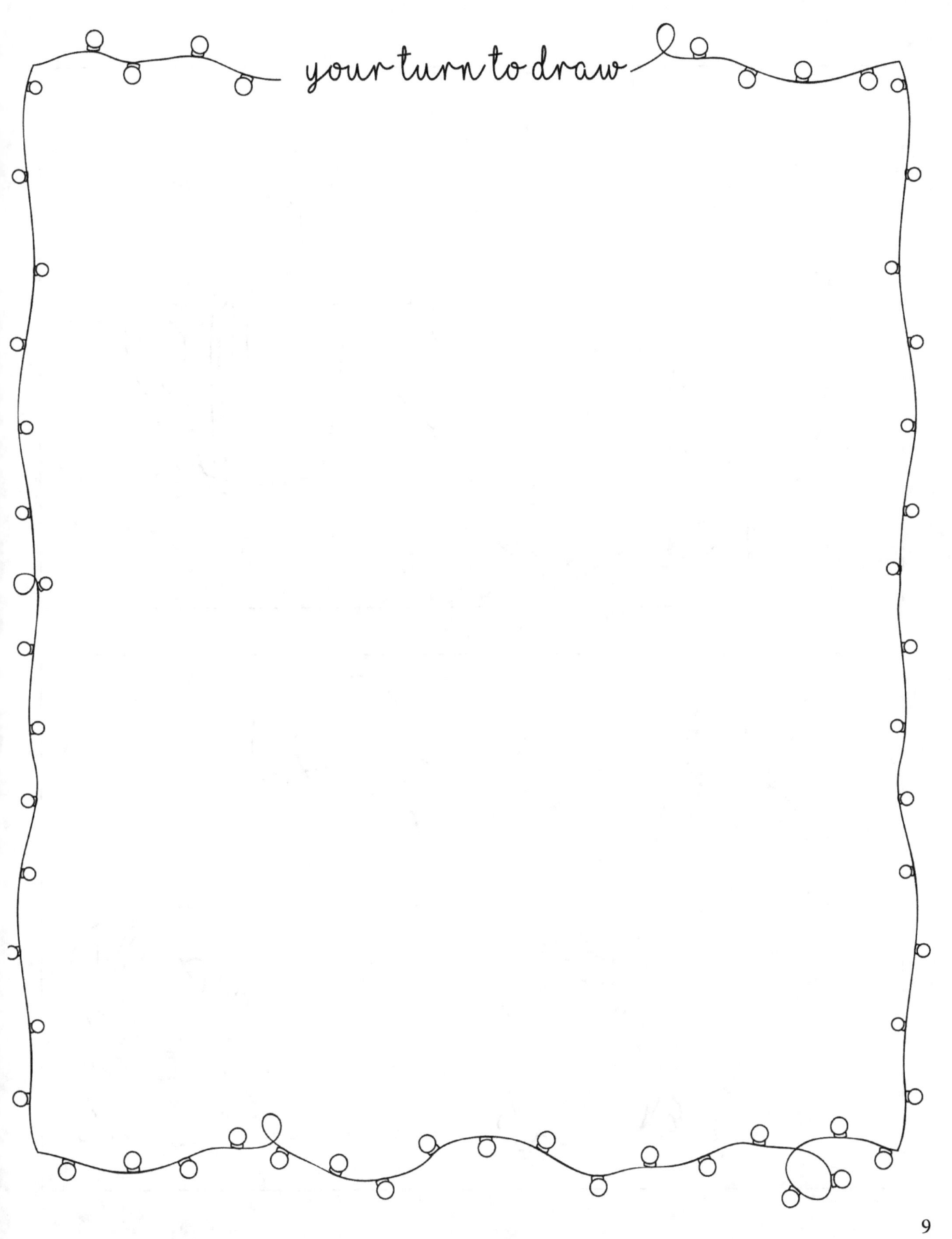

your turn to draw

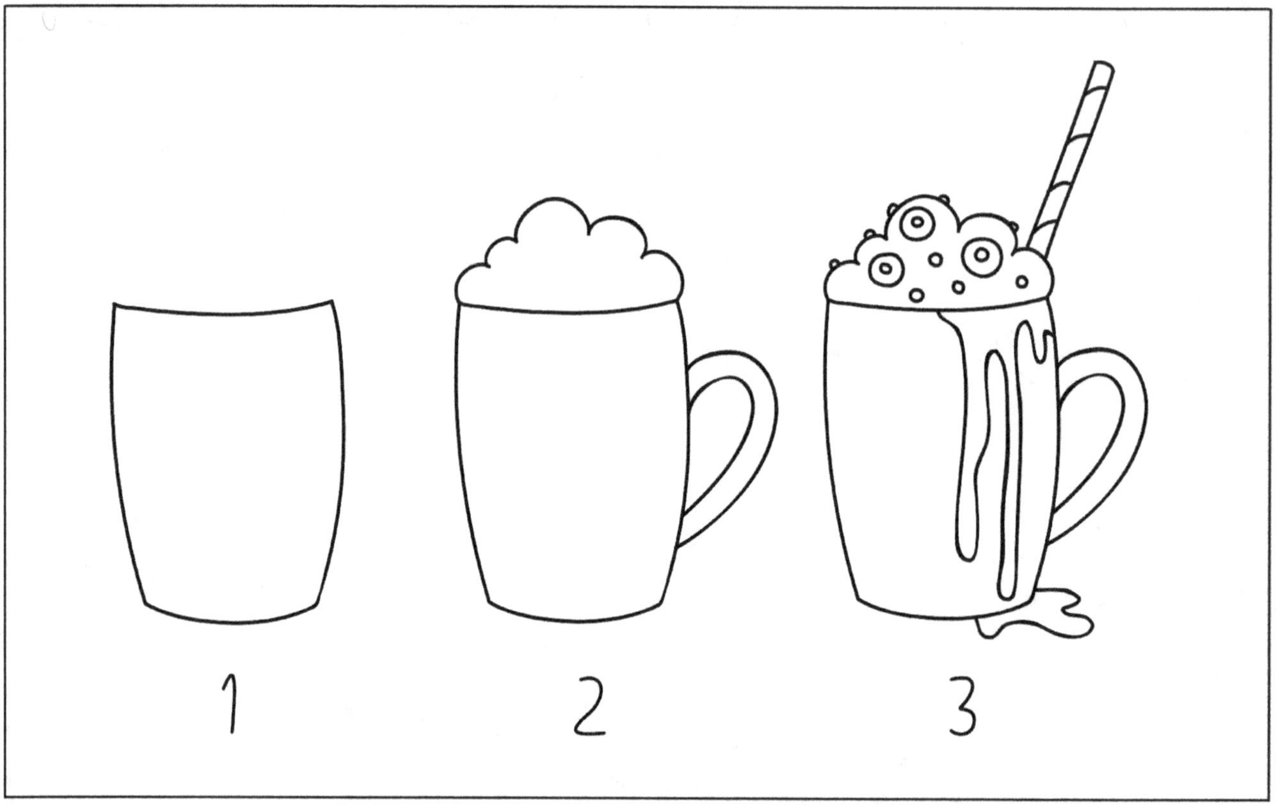

1

2

3

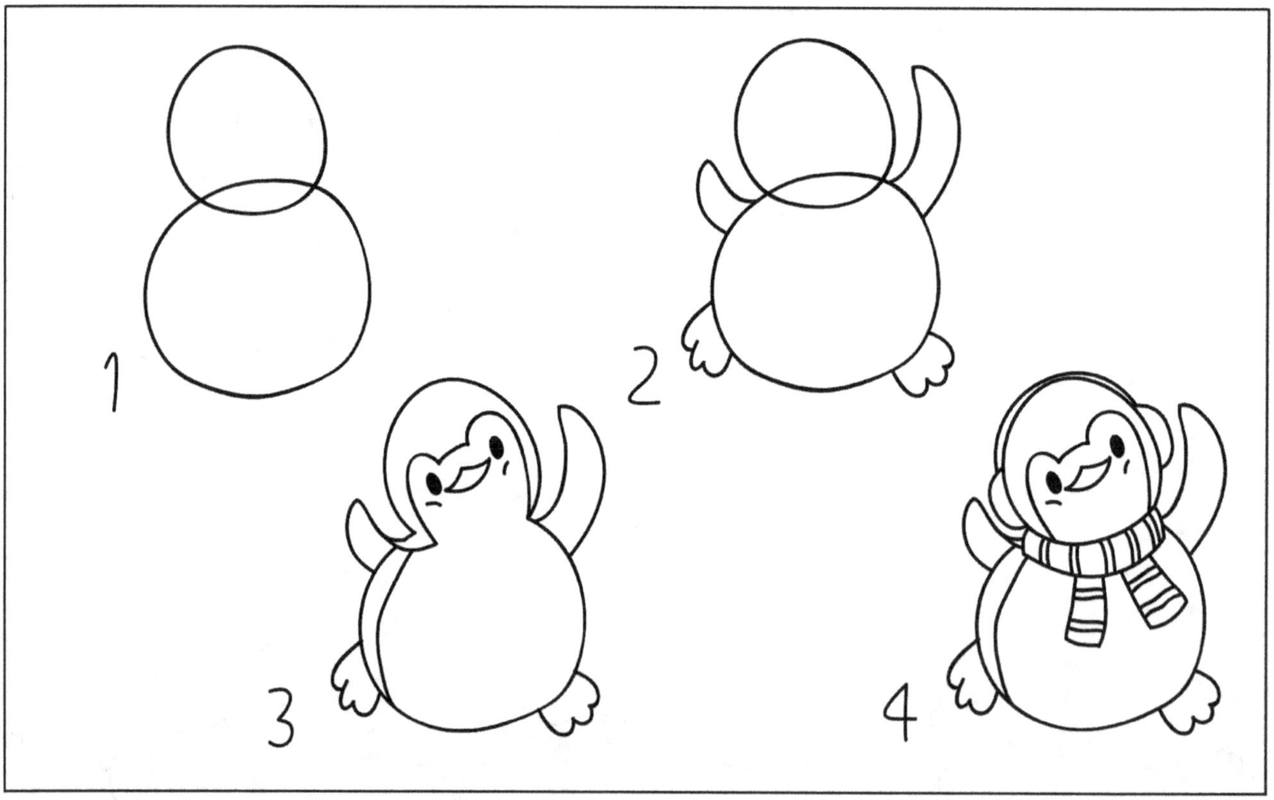

1

2

3

4

10

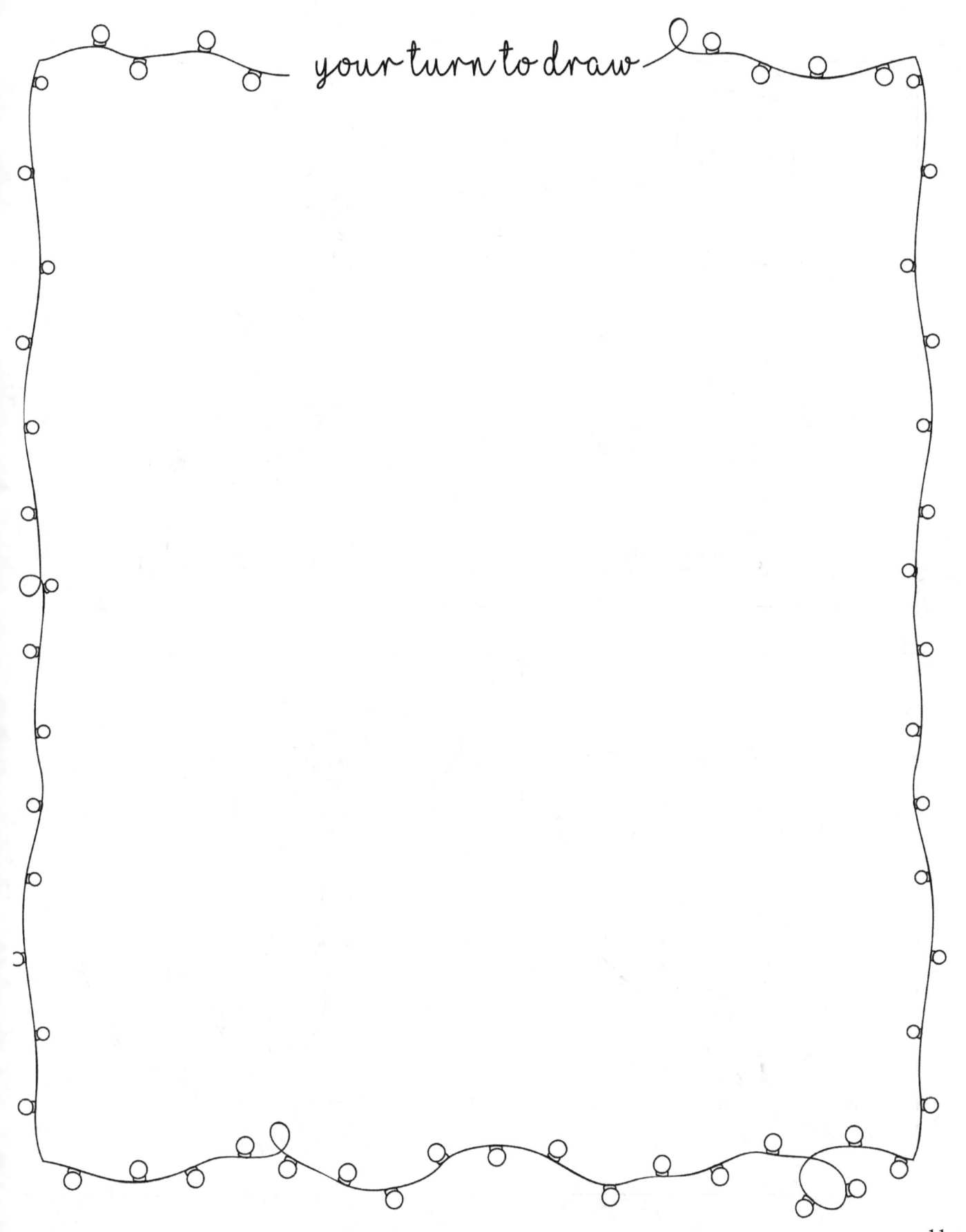

your turn to draw

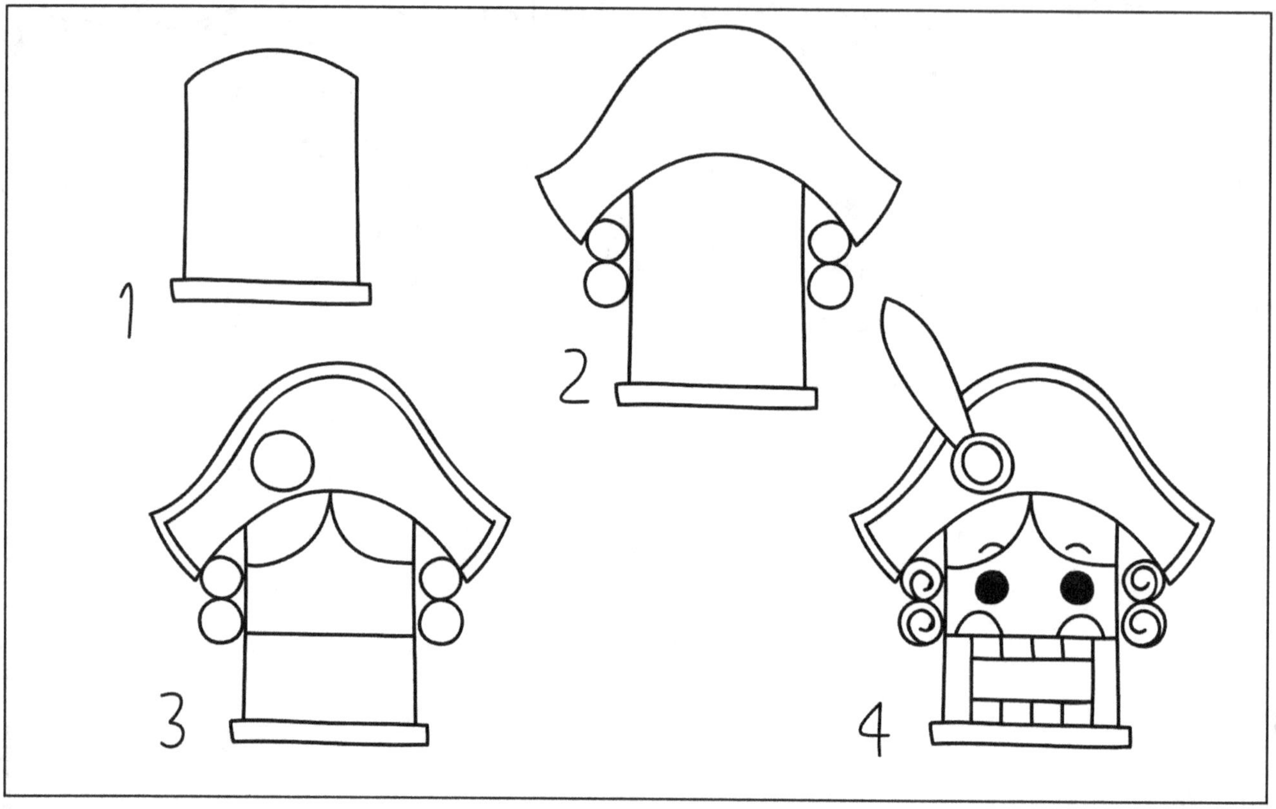

1

2

3

4

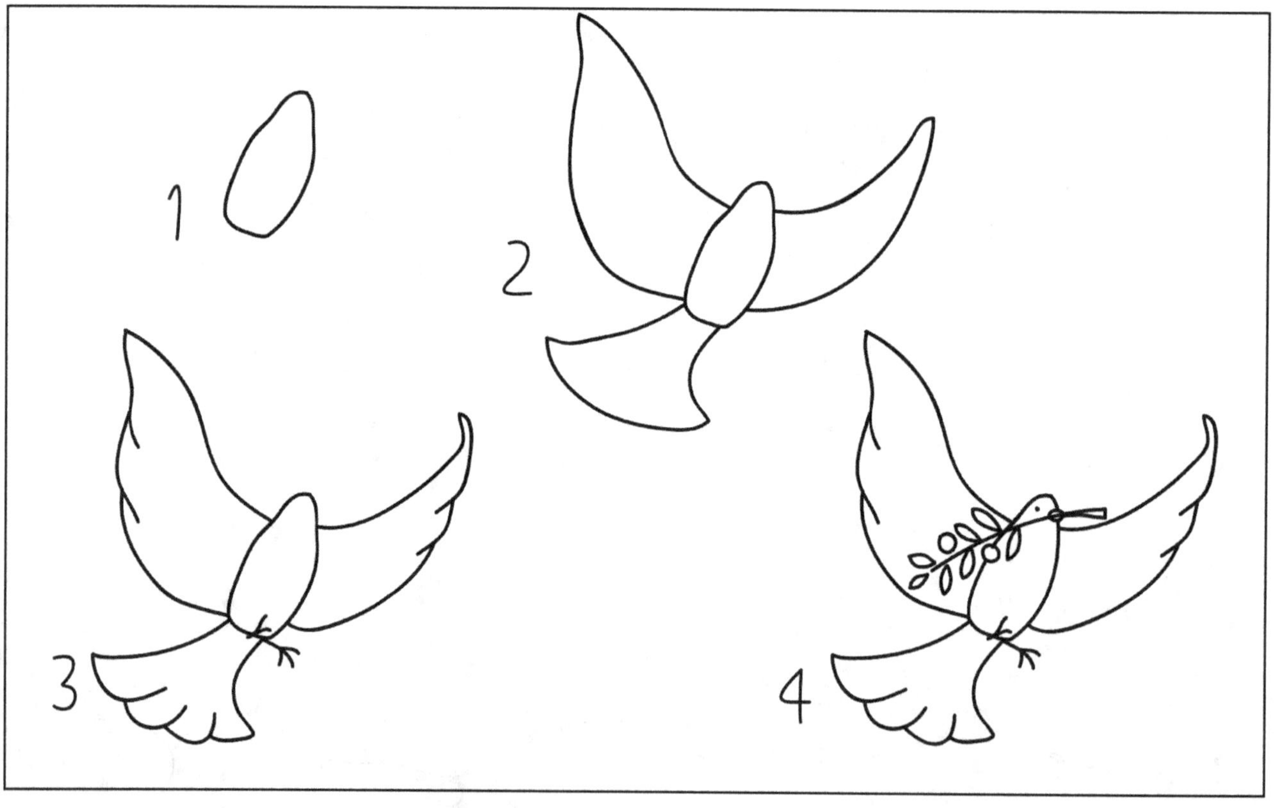

1

2

3

4

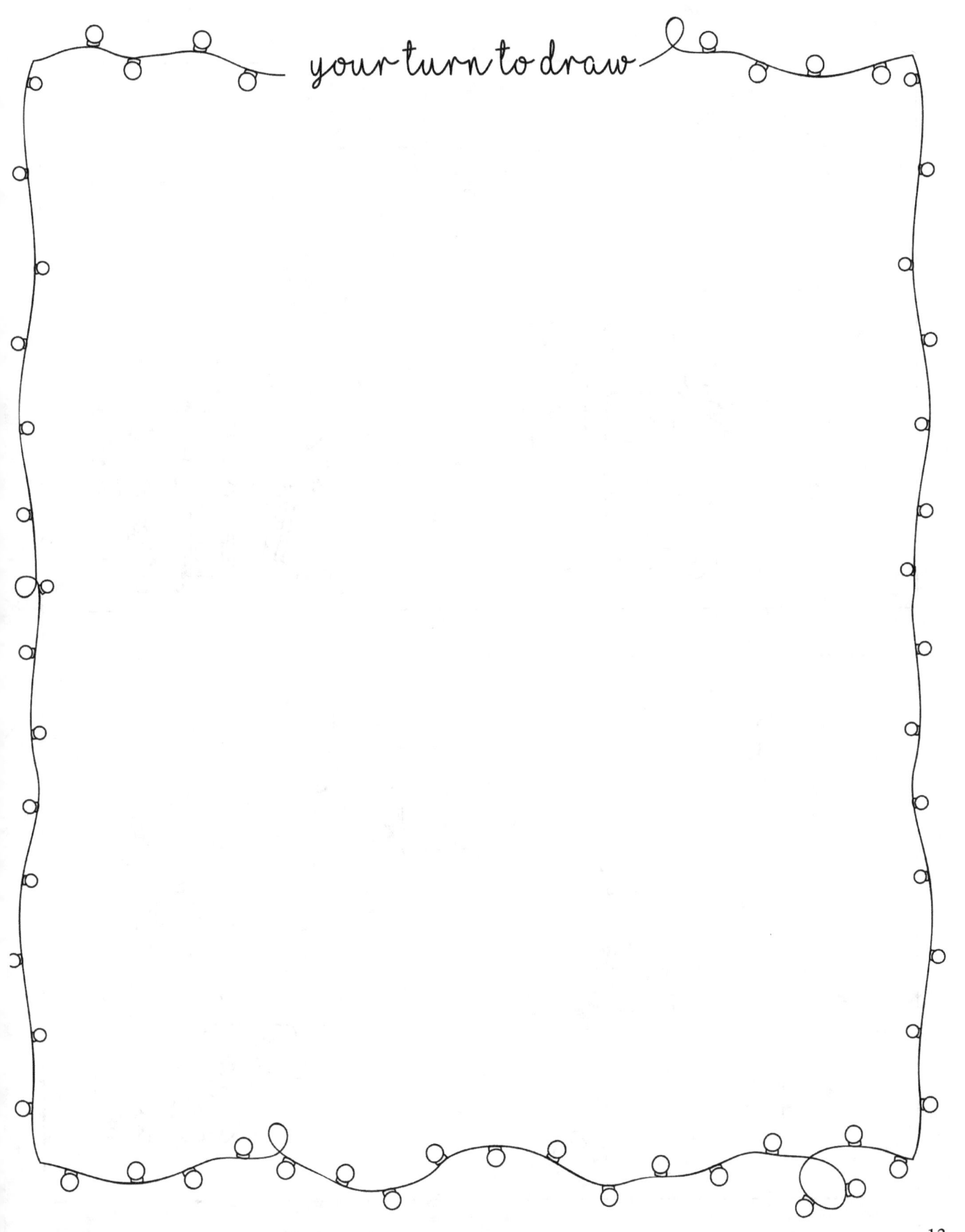

your turn to draw

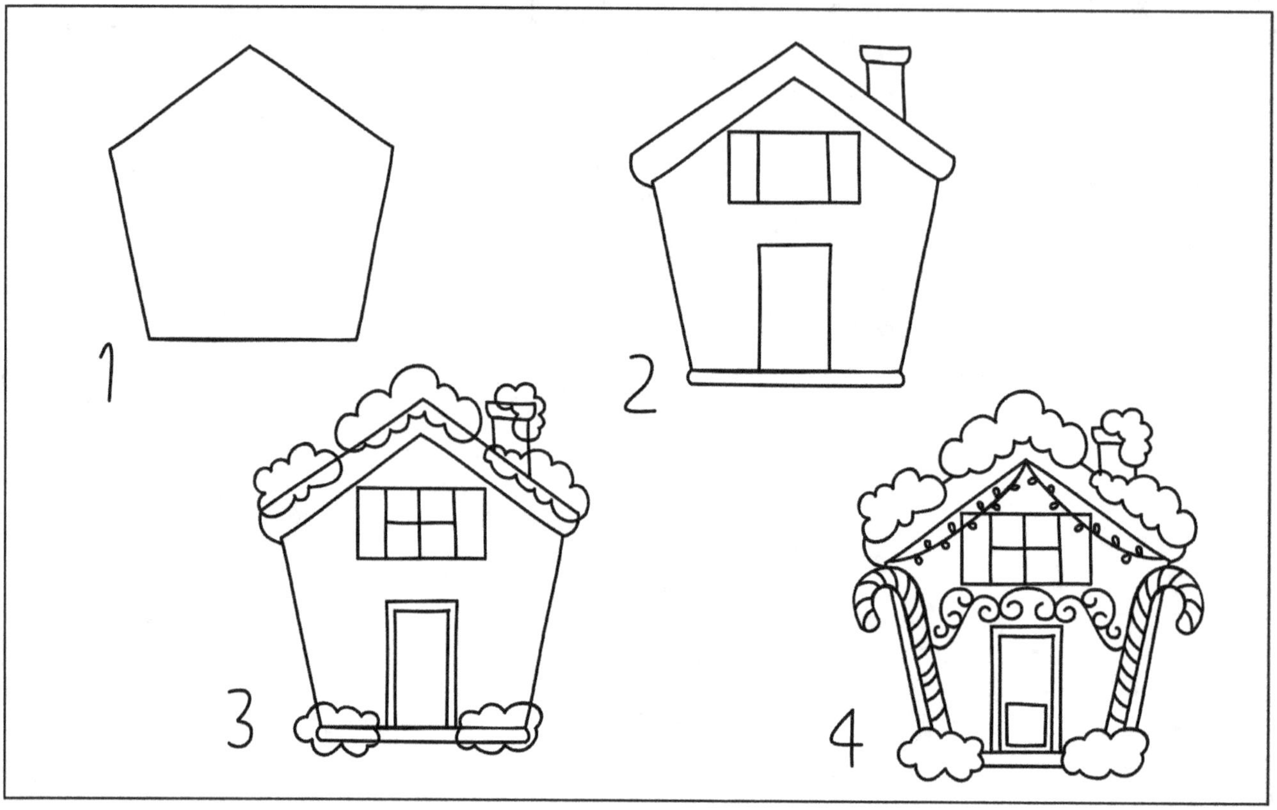

1

2

3

4

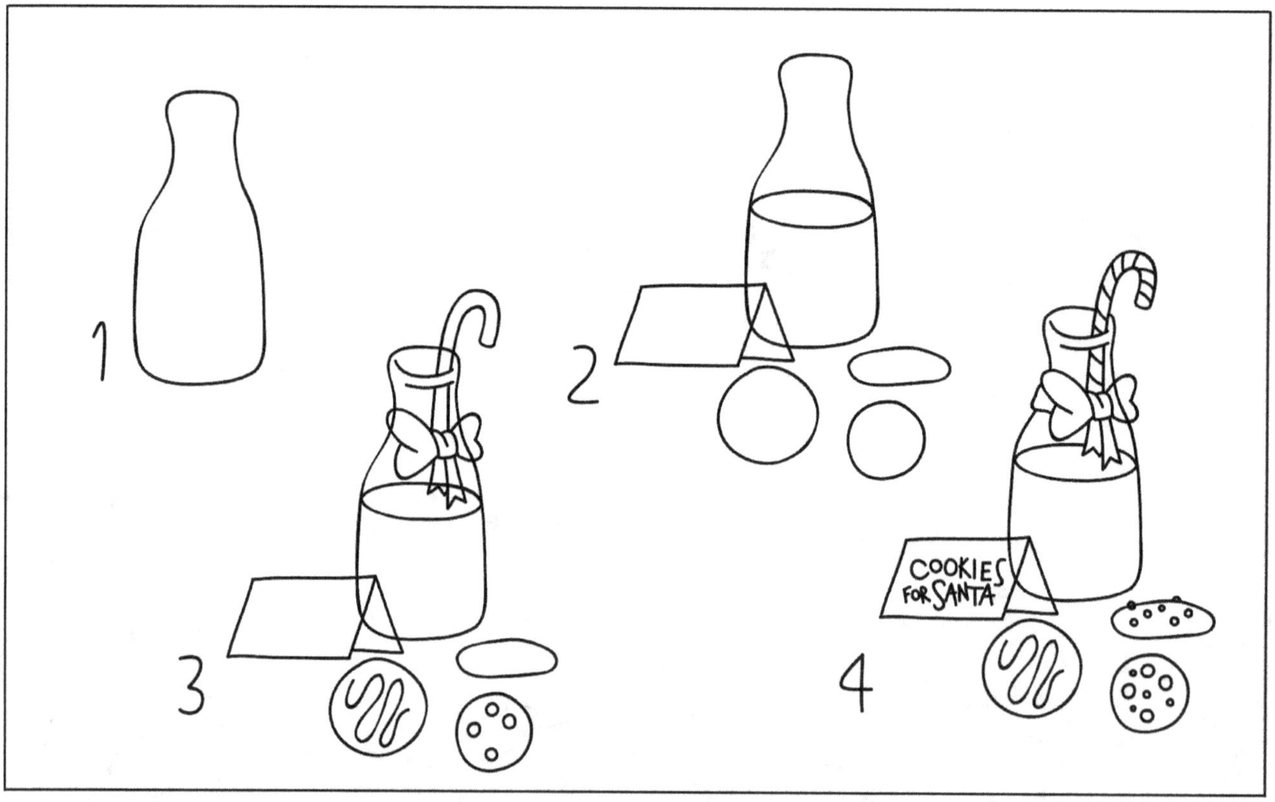

1

2

3

4

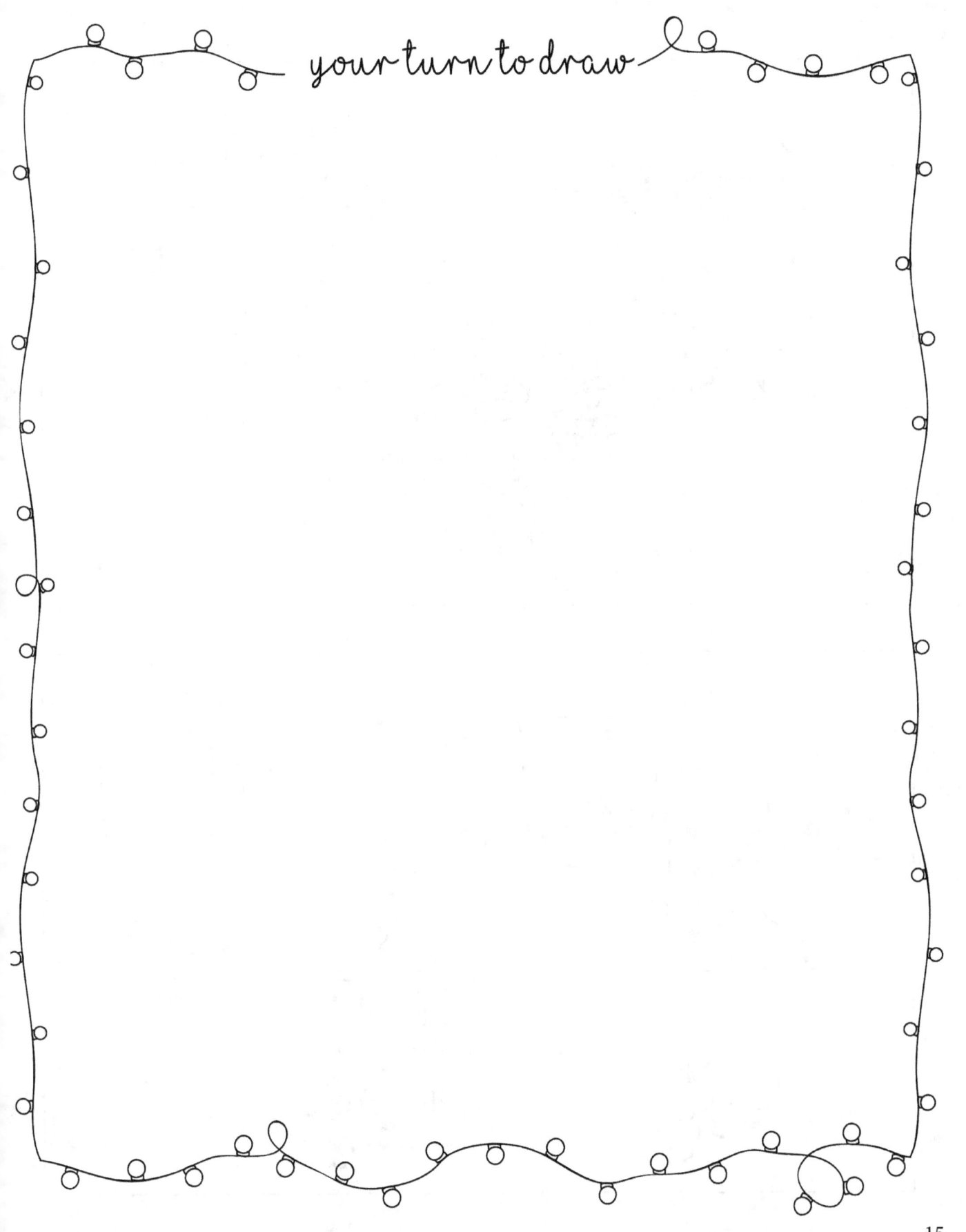

your turn to draw

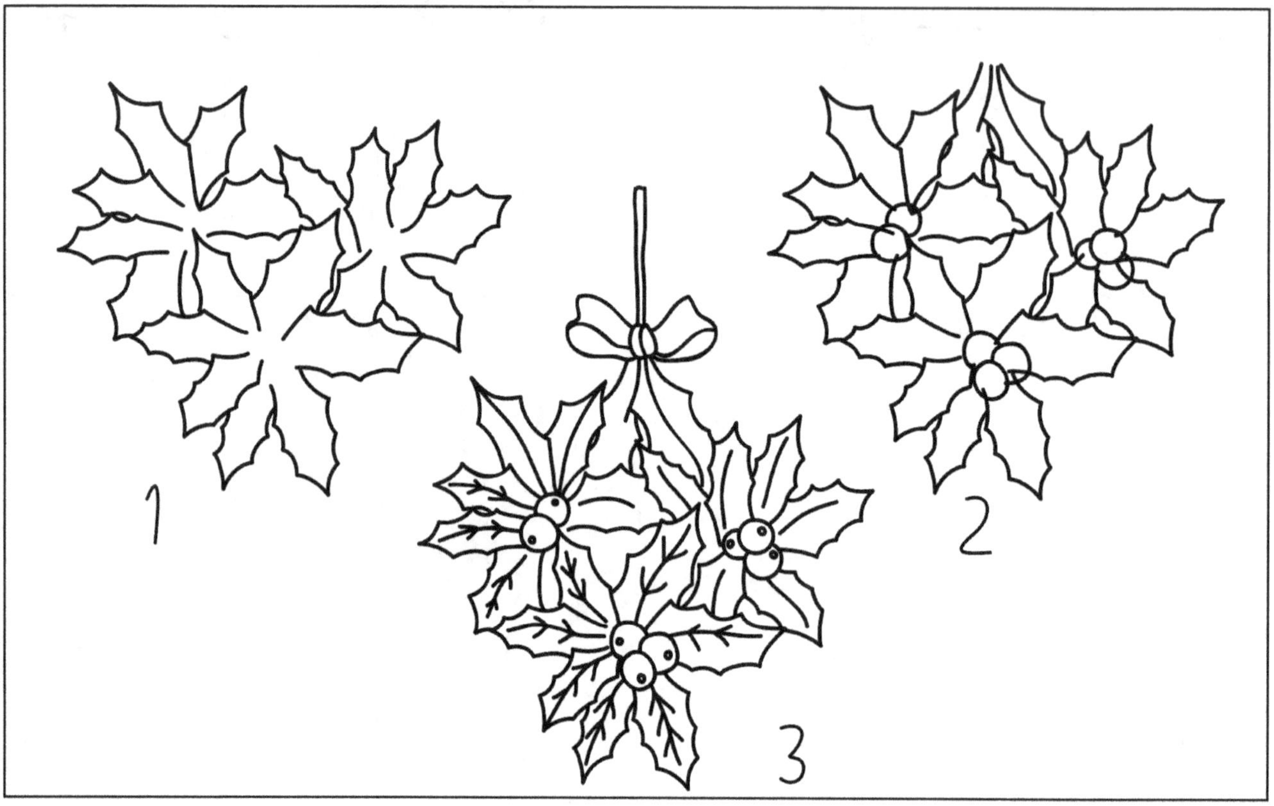

1

2

3

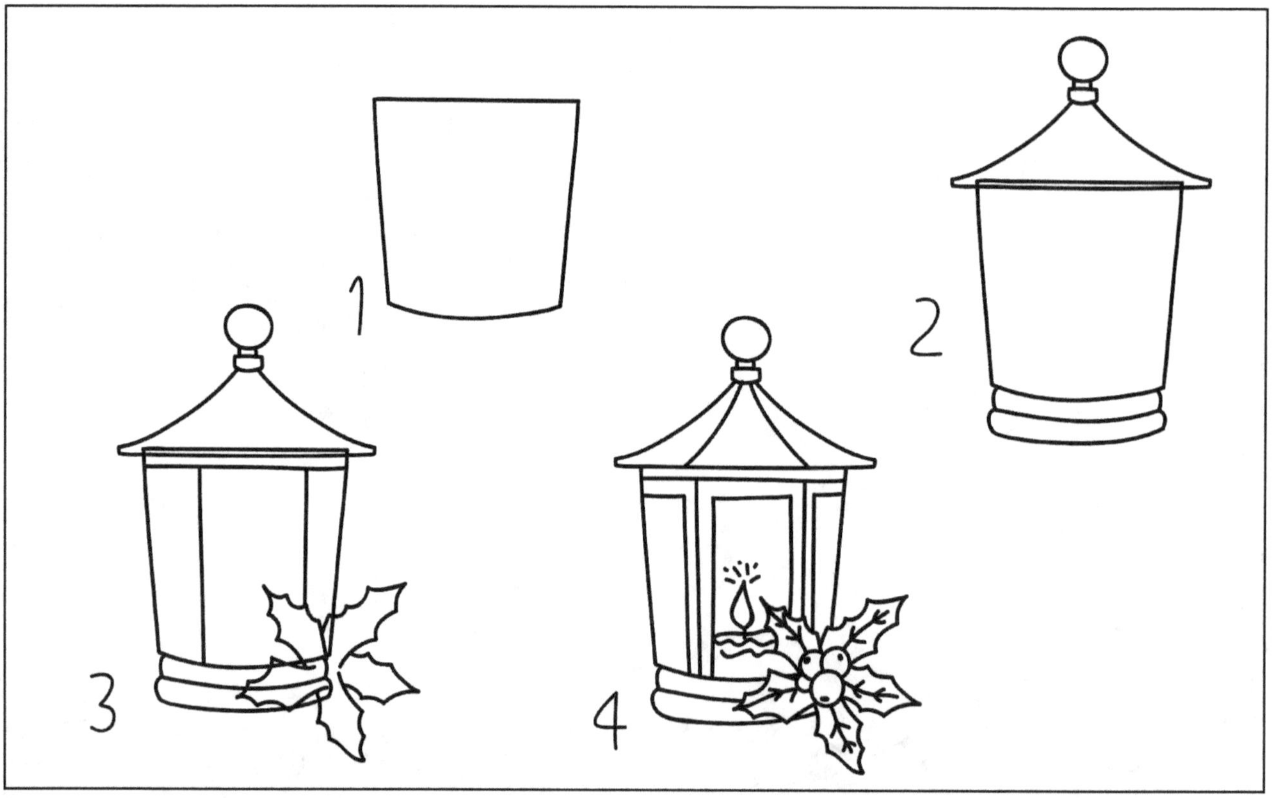

1

2

3

4

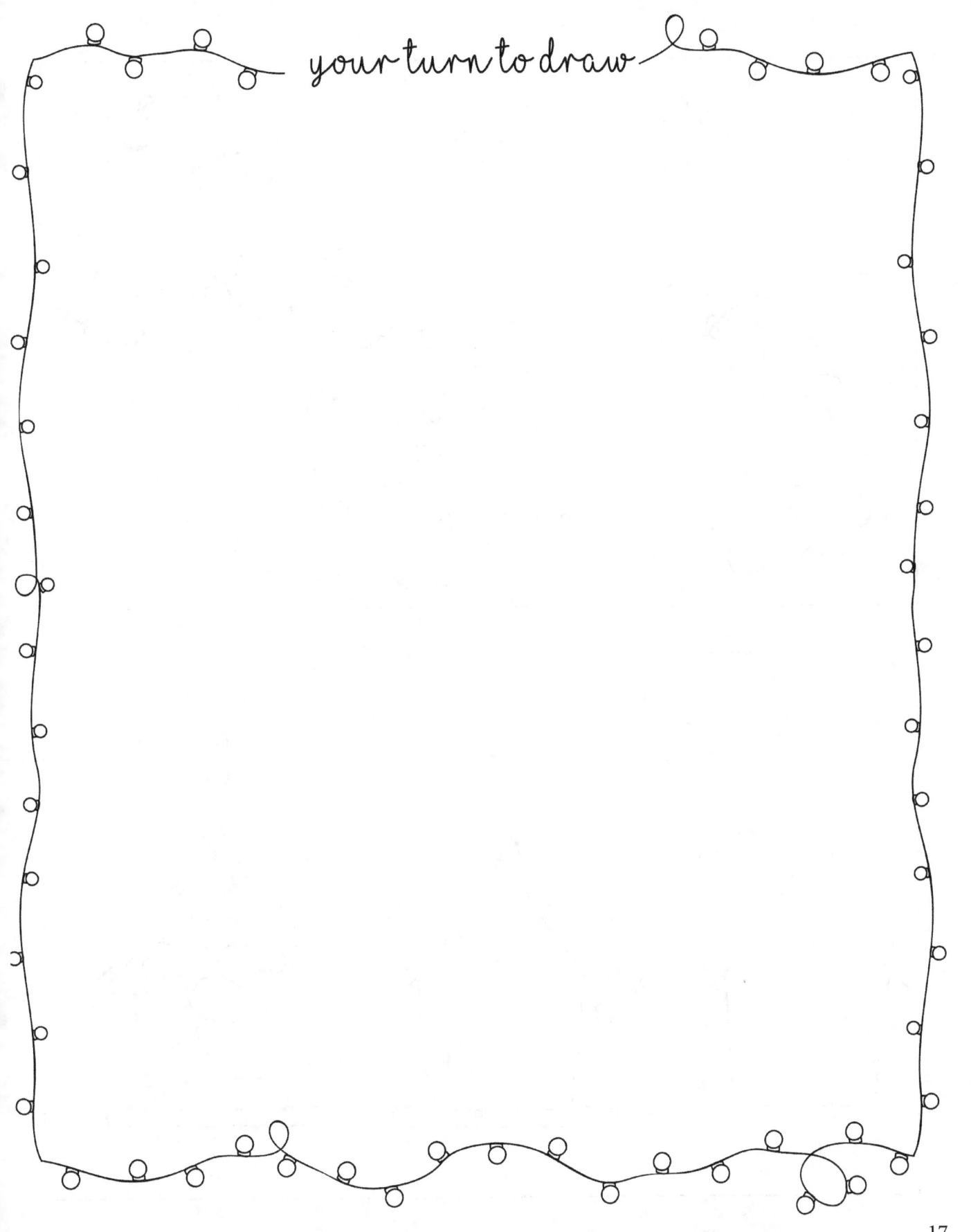

your turn to draw

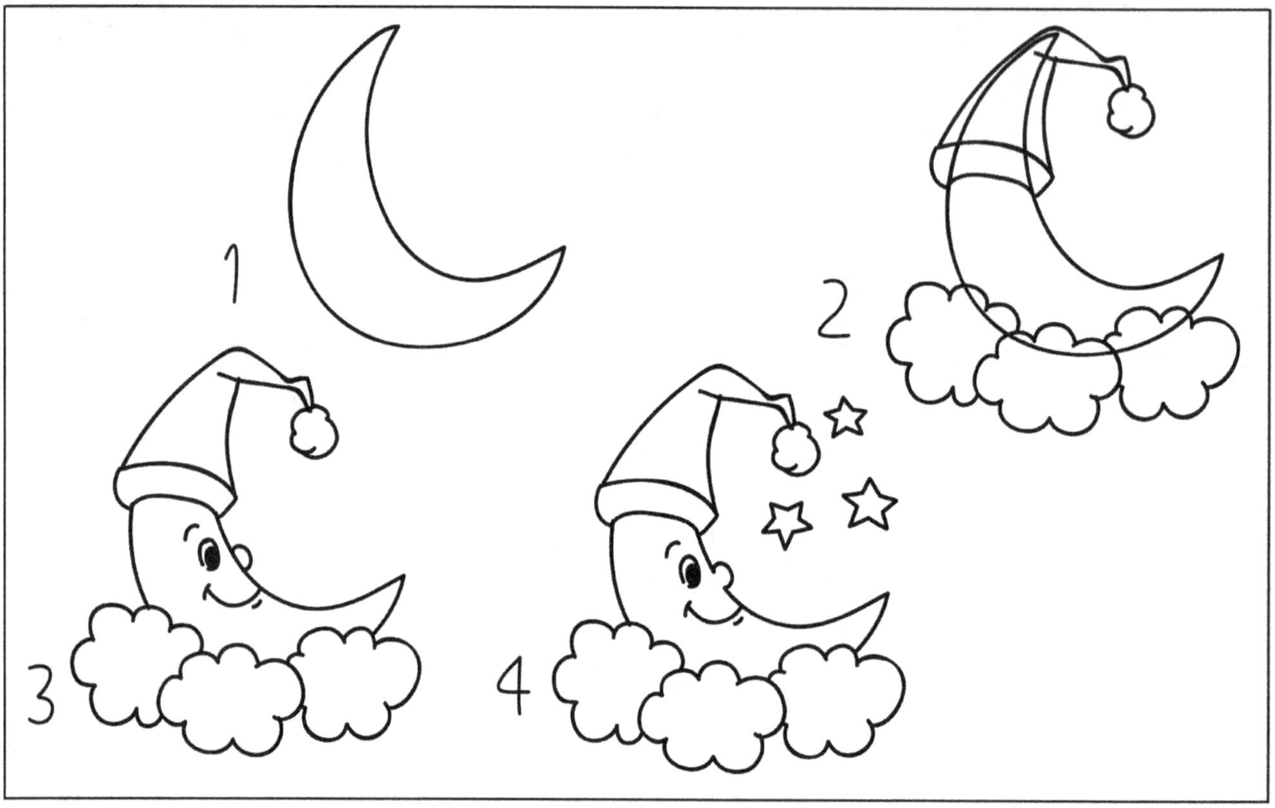

1

2

3

4

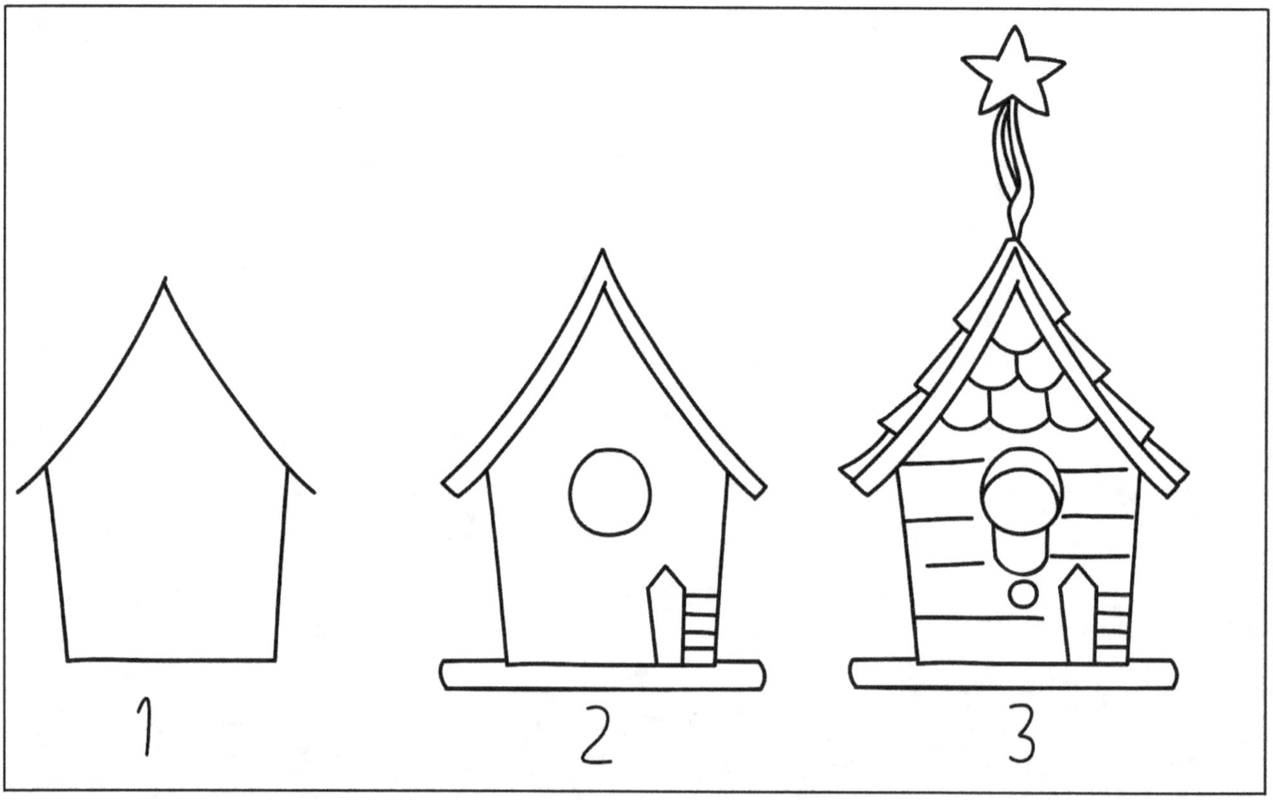

1

2

3

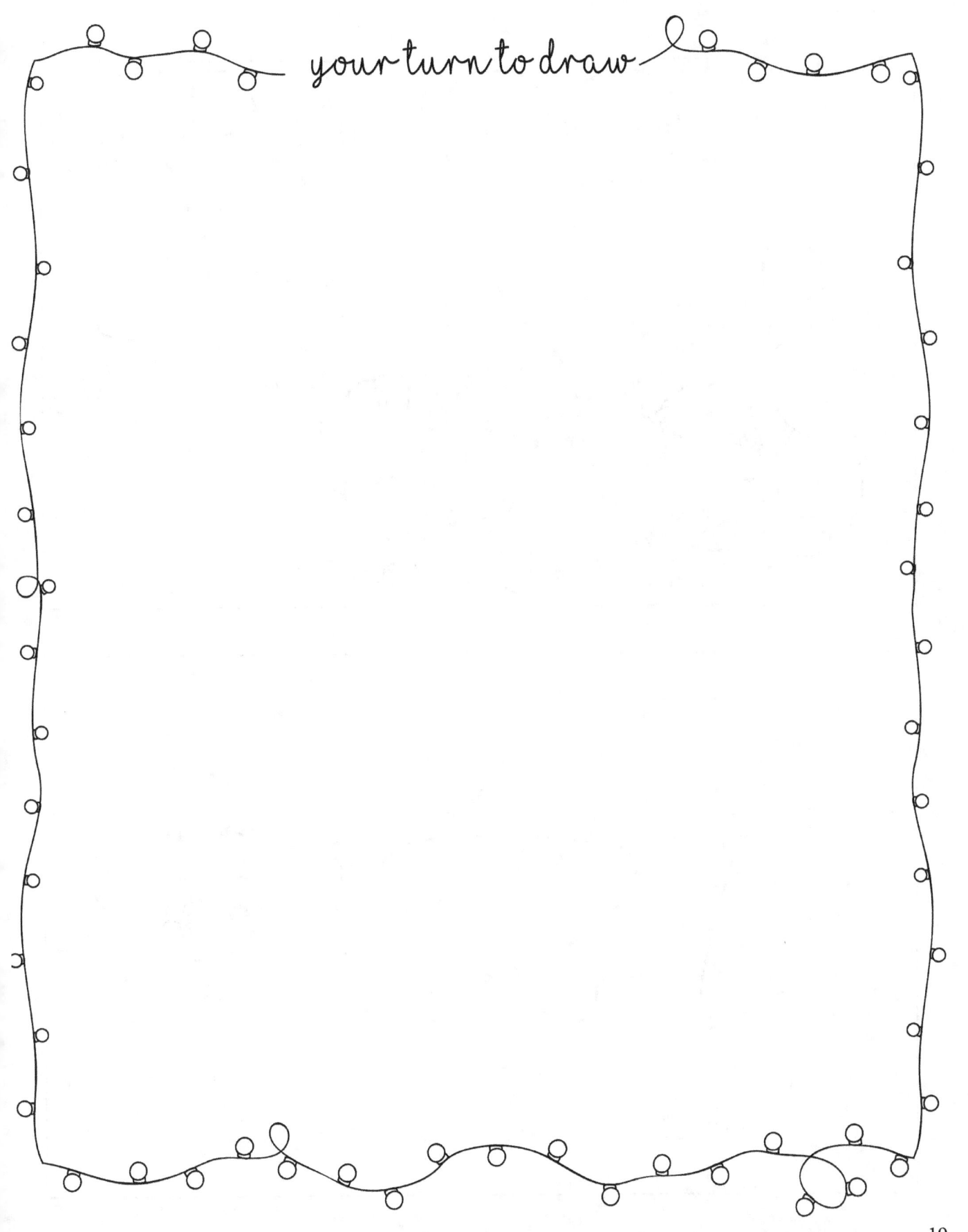

your turn to draw

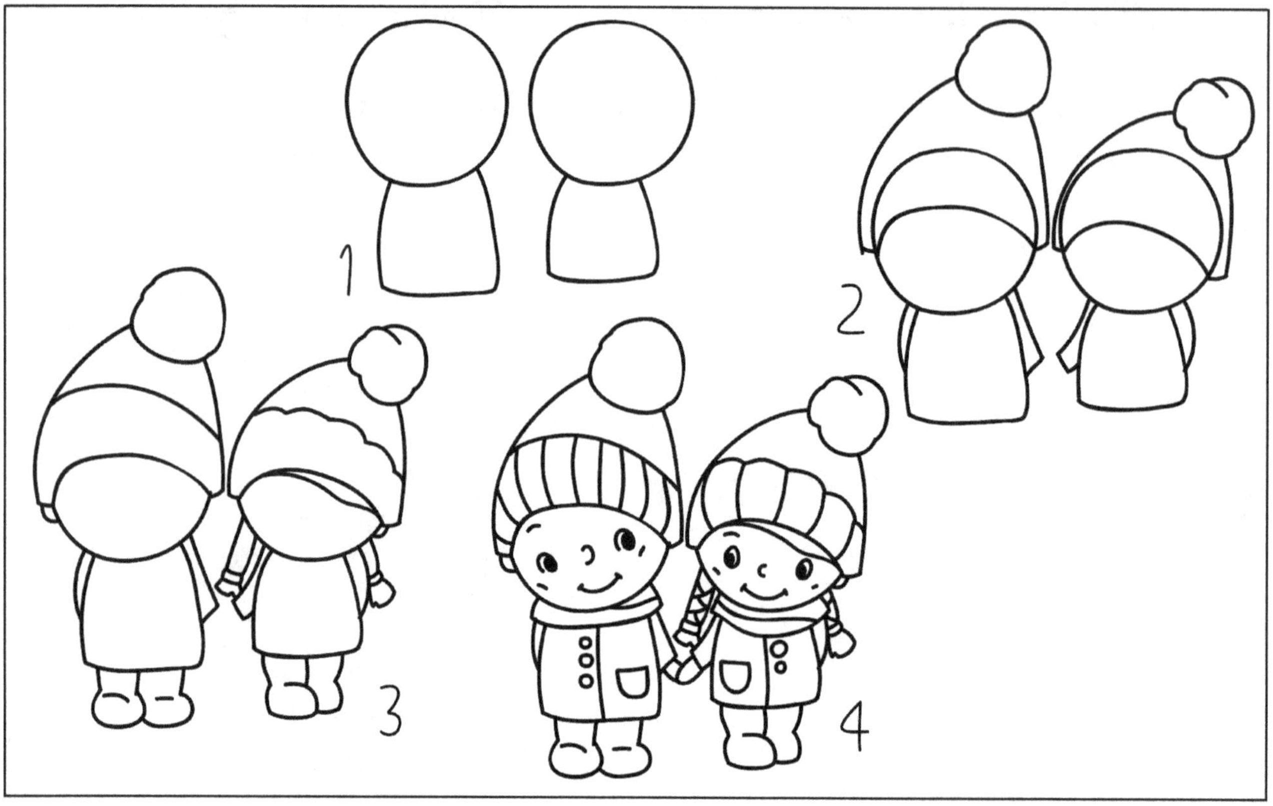

1

2

3

4

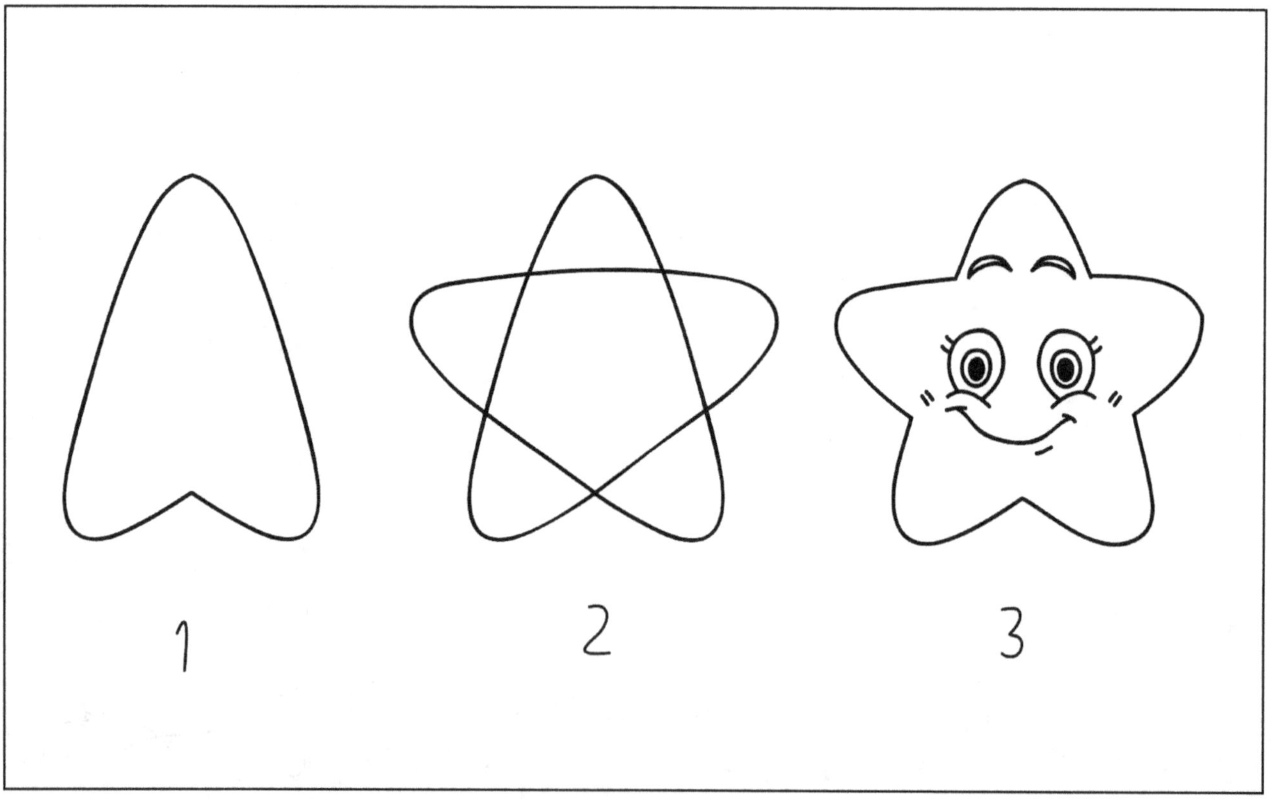

1

2

3

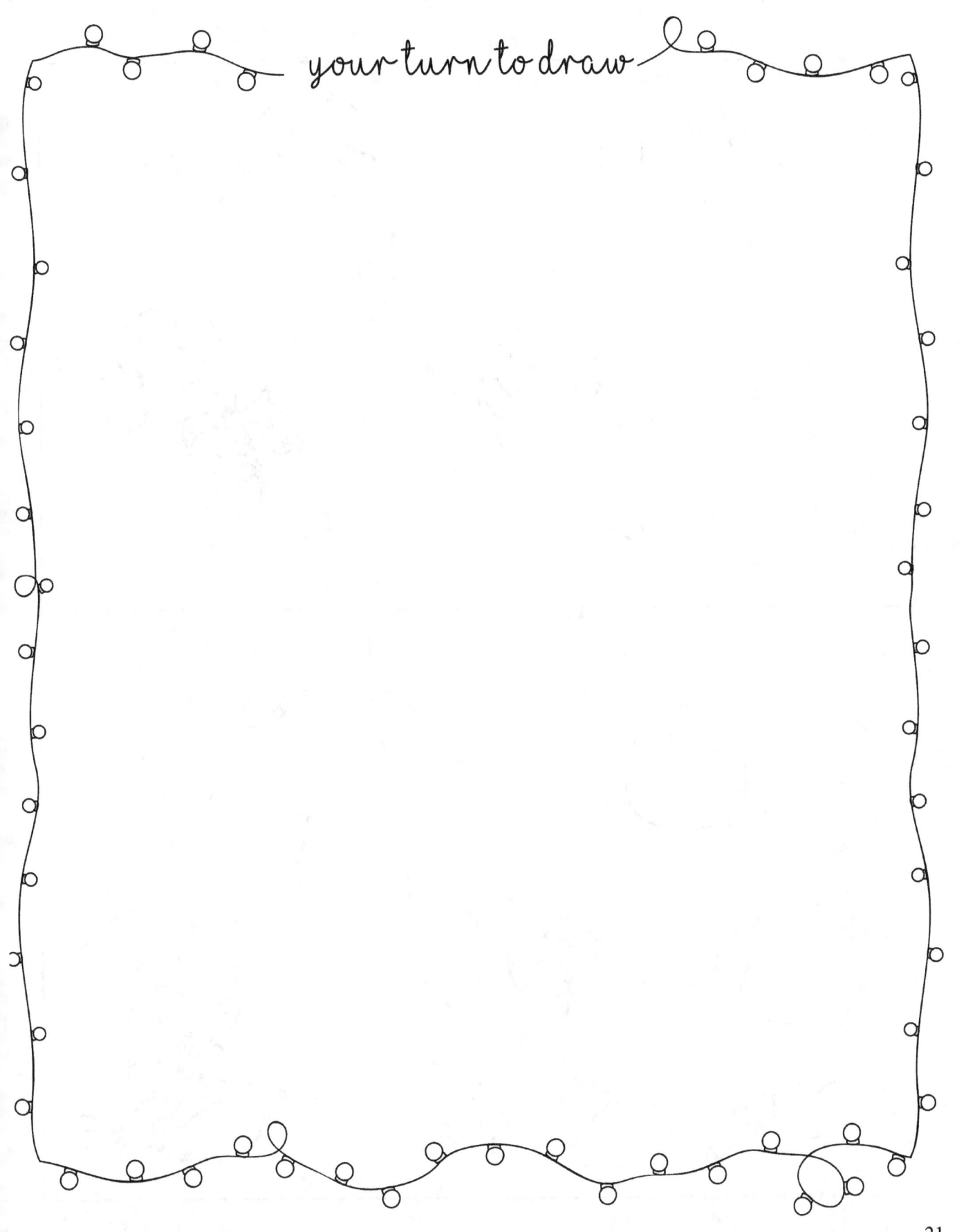

your turn to draw

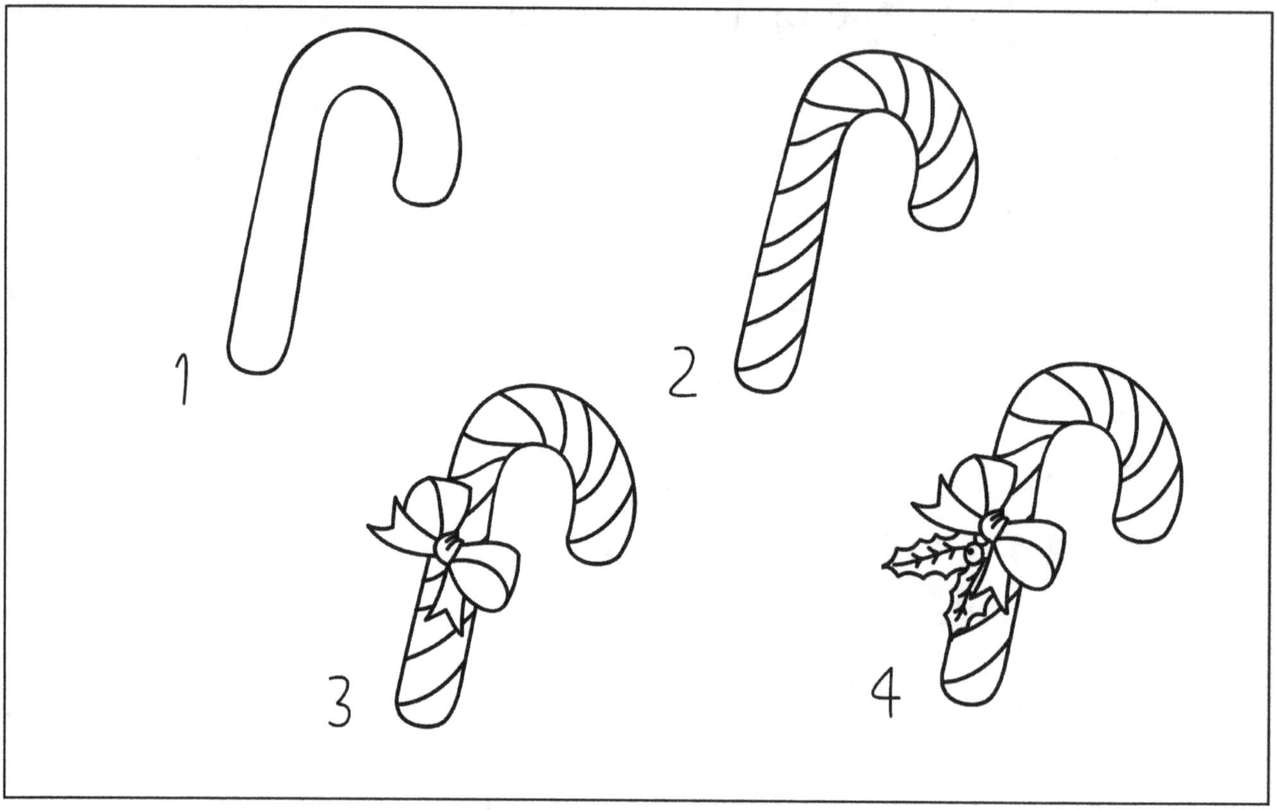

1

2

3

4

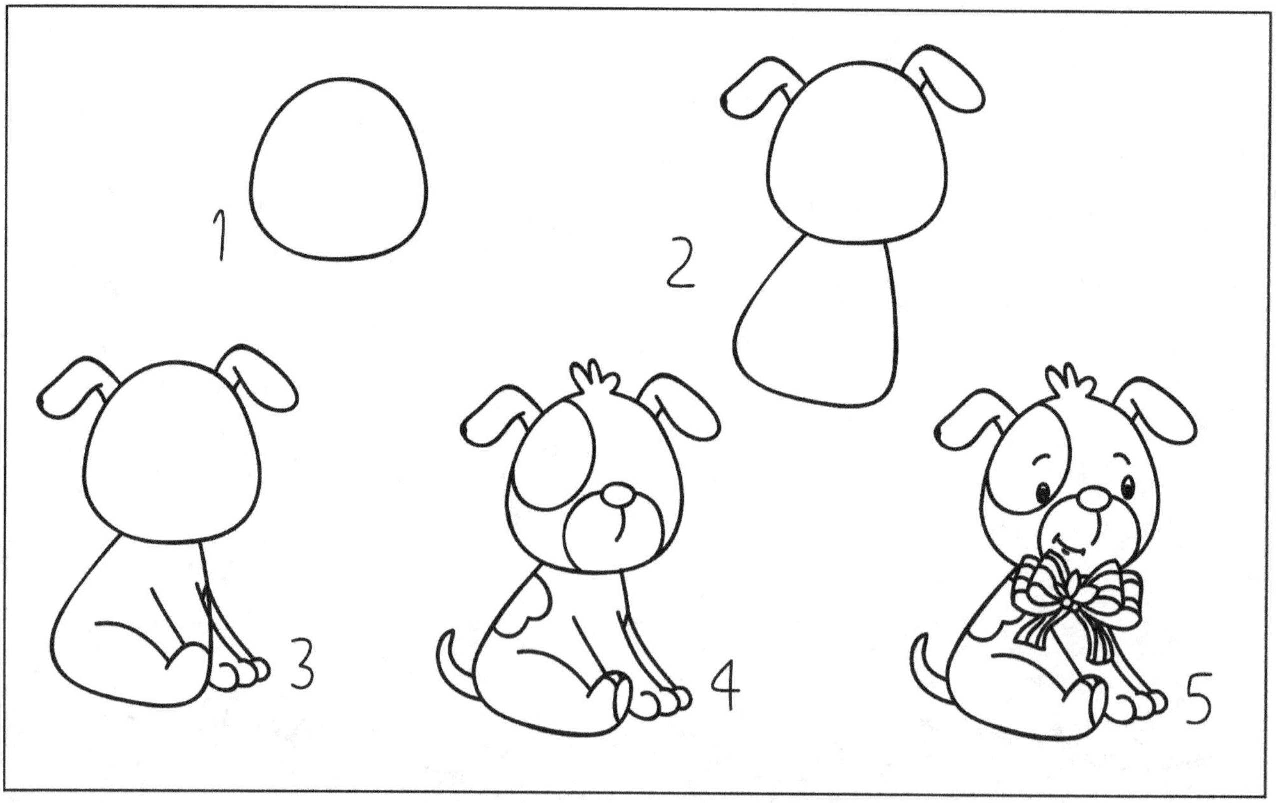

1

2

3

4

5

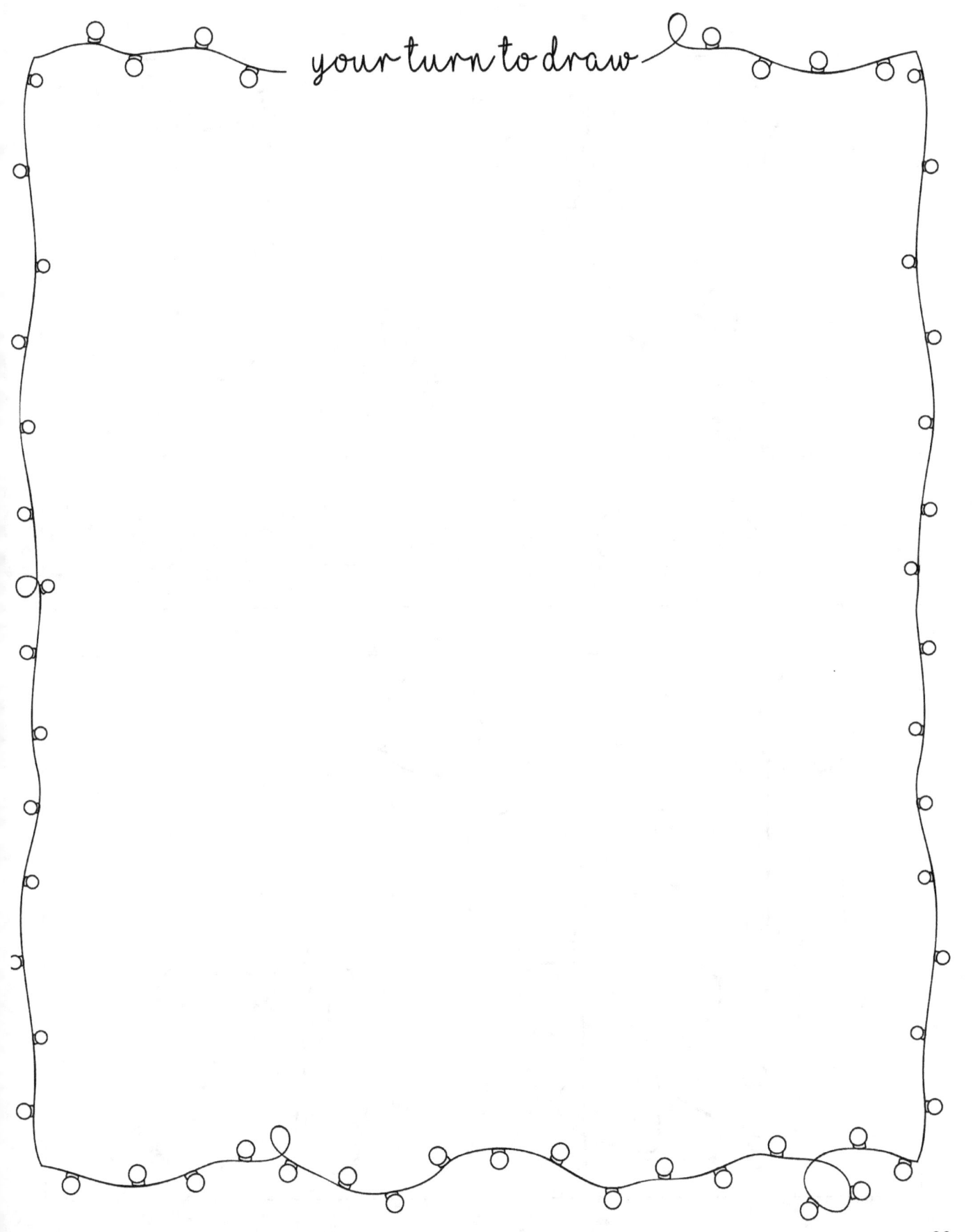

your turn to draw

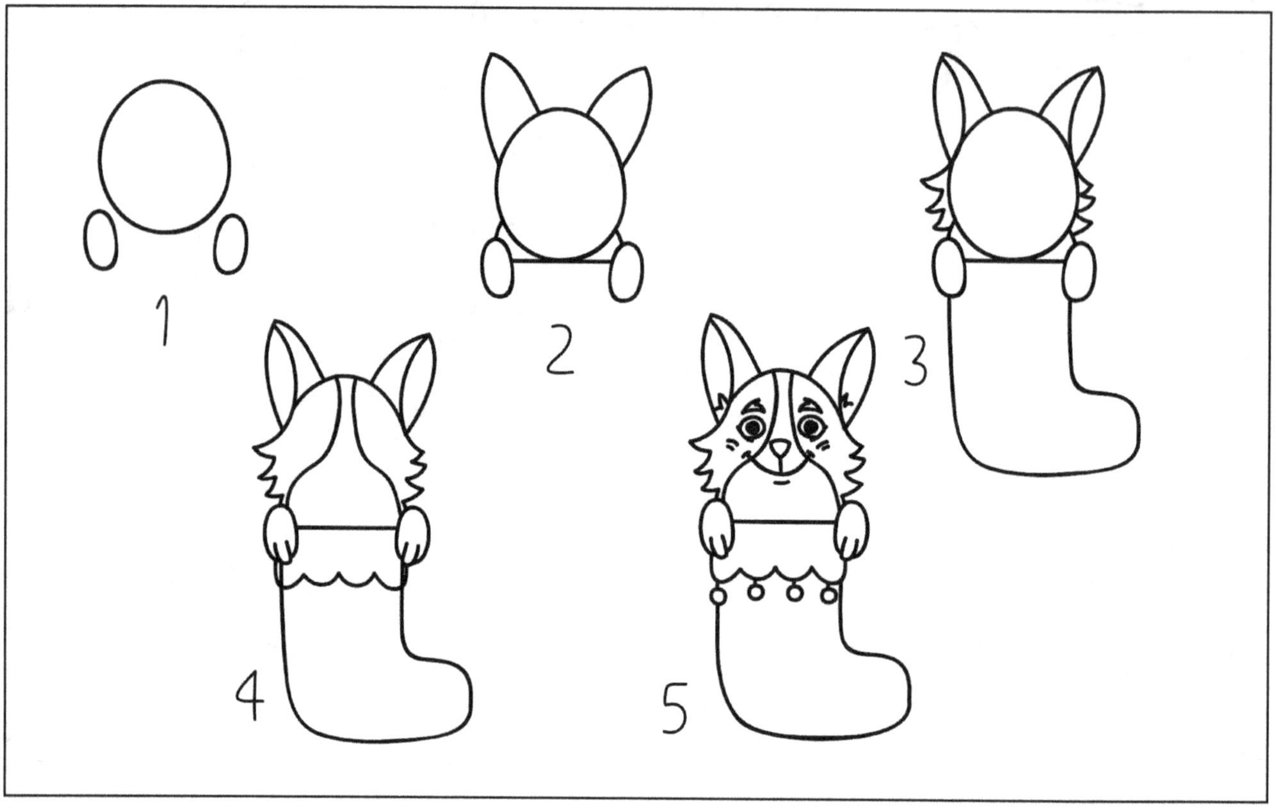

1

2

3

4

5

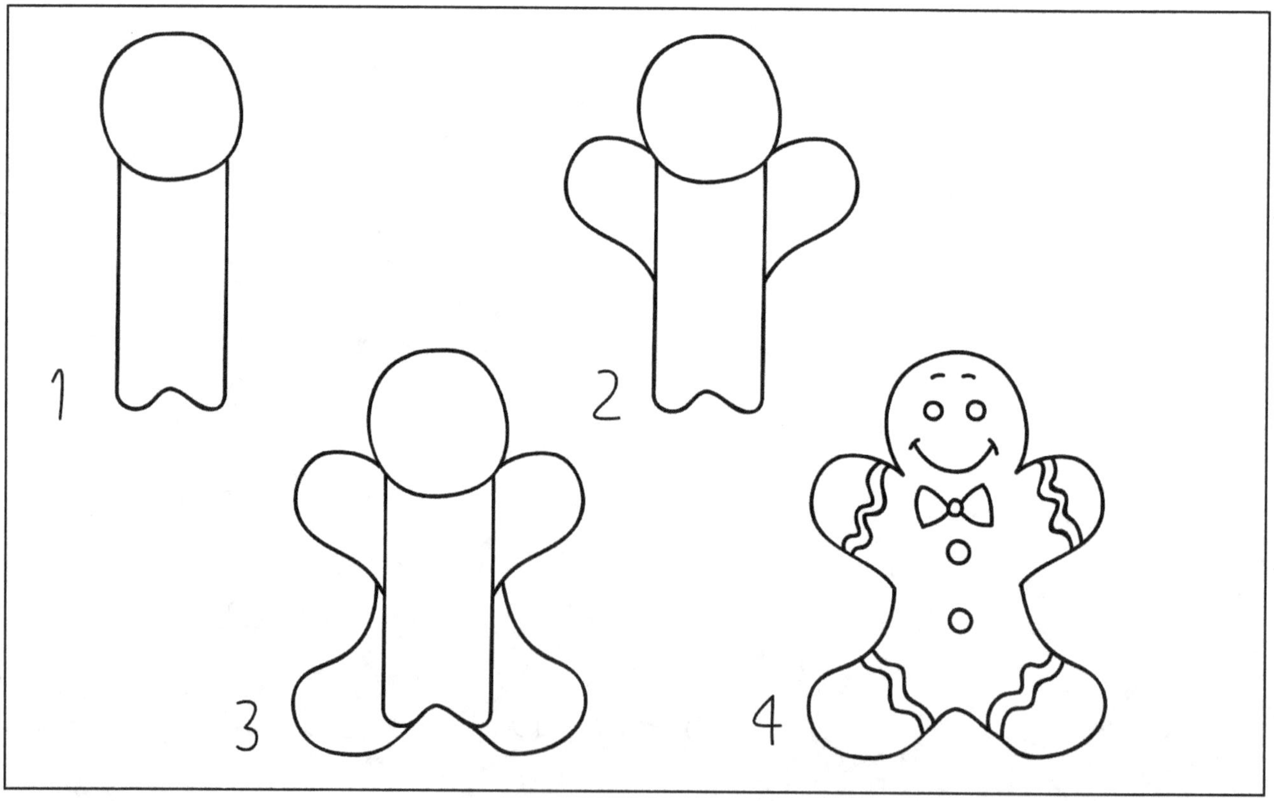

1

2

3

4

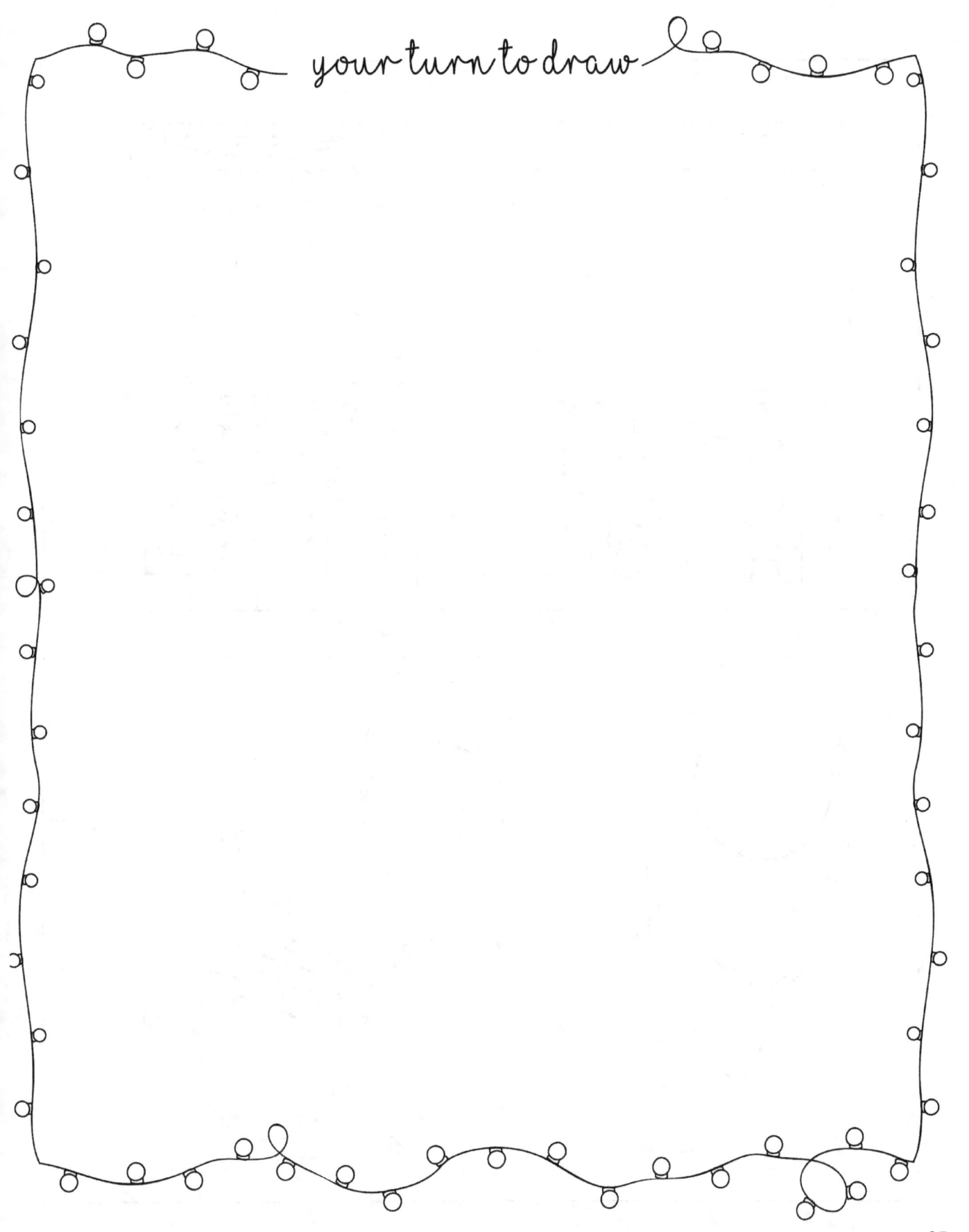

your turn to draw

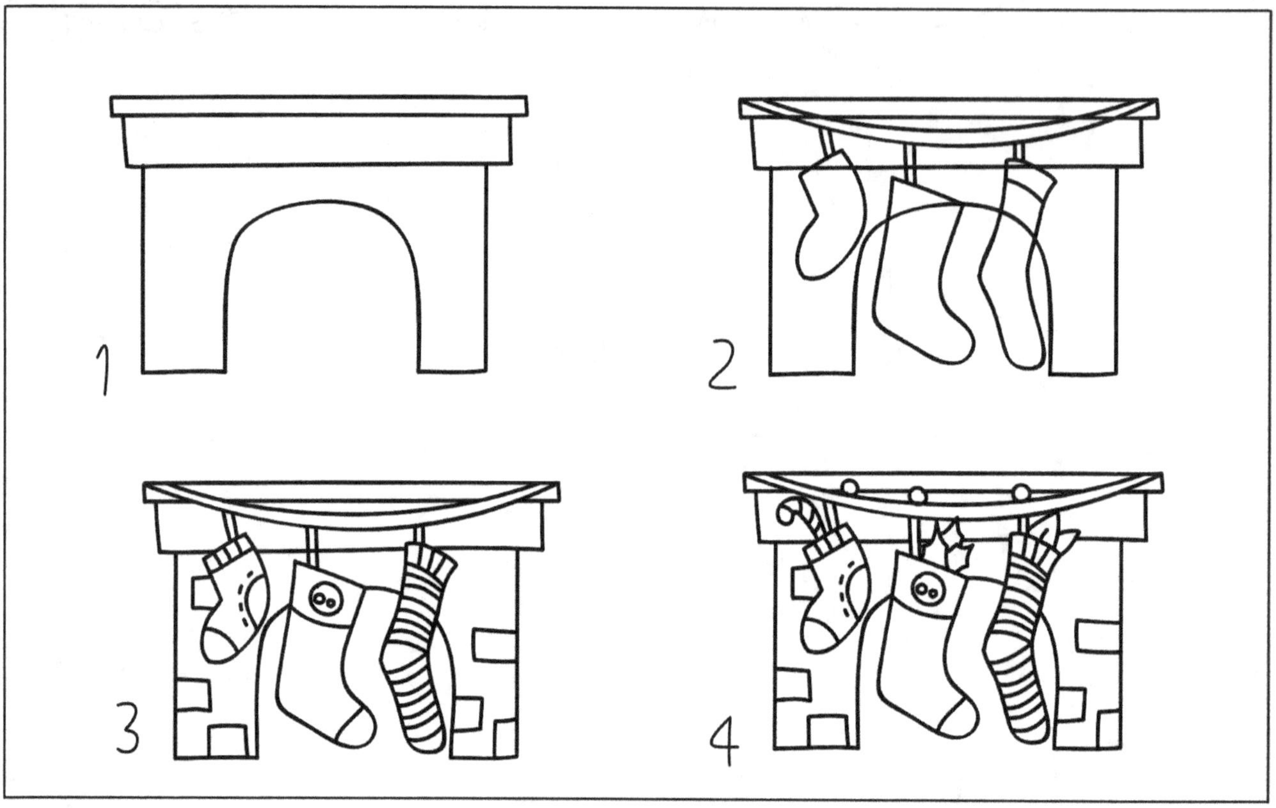

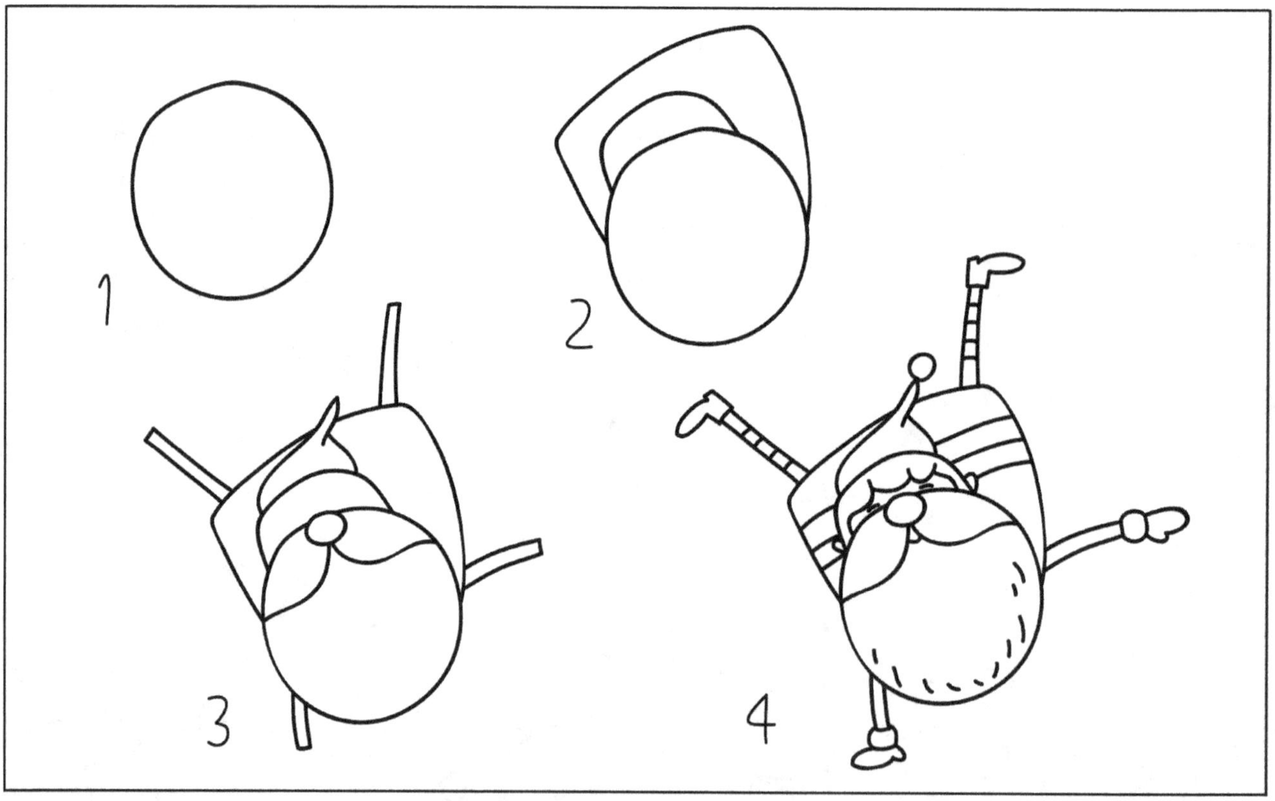

1

2

3

4

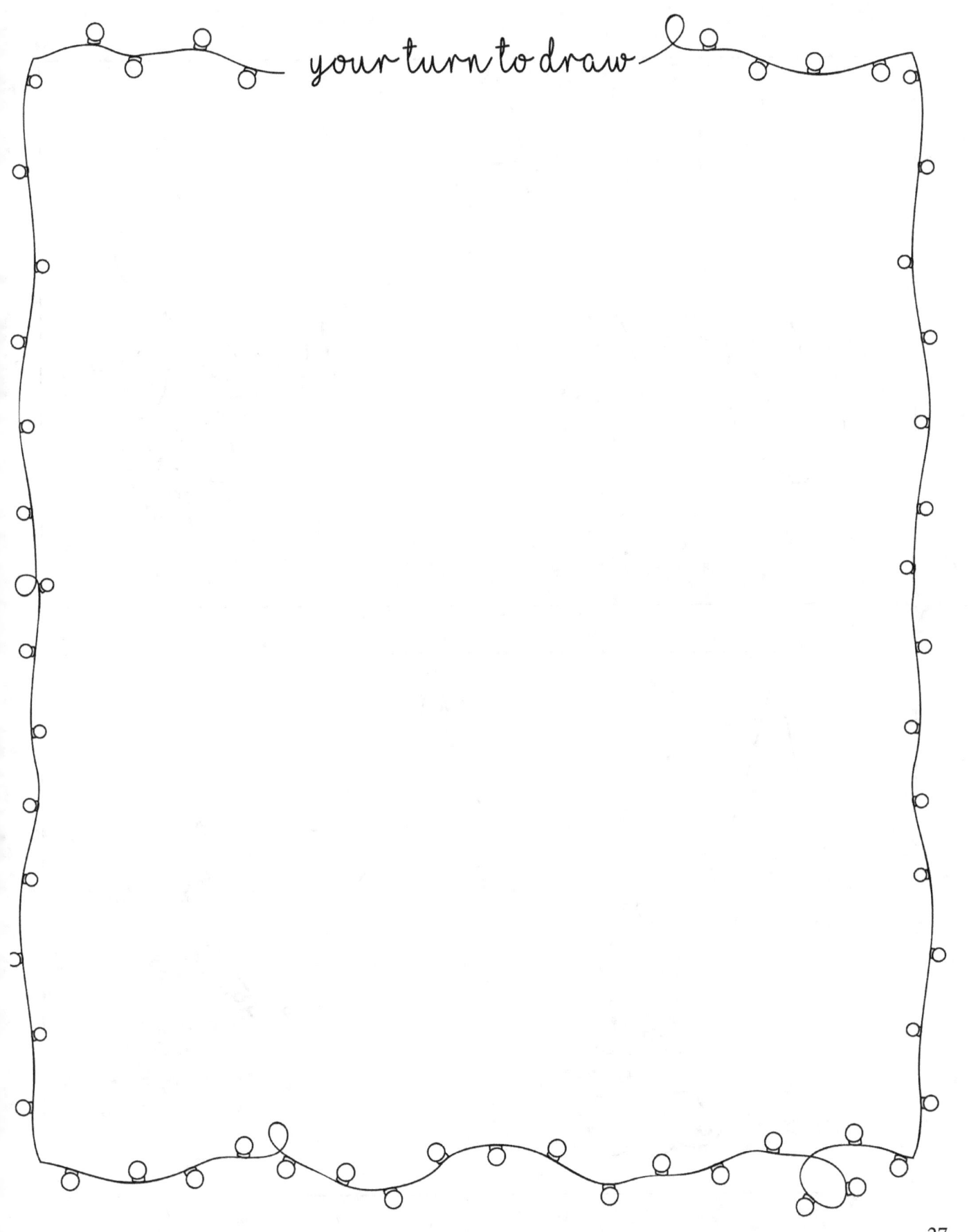

your turn to draw

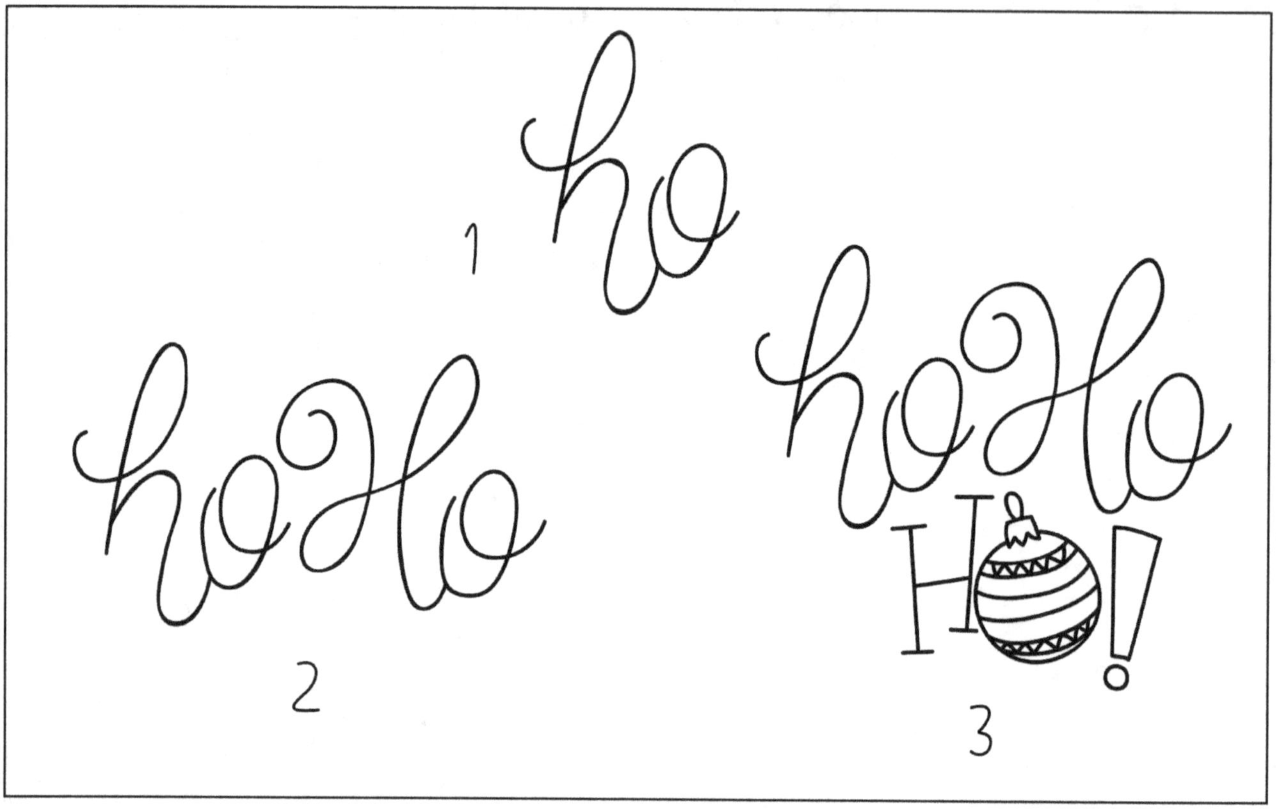

ho

1

ho ho

2

ho ho ho

HO!

3

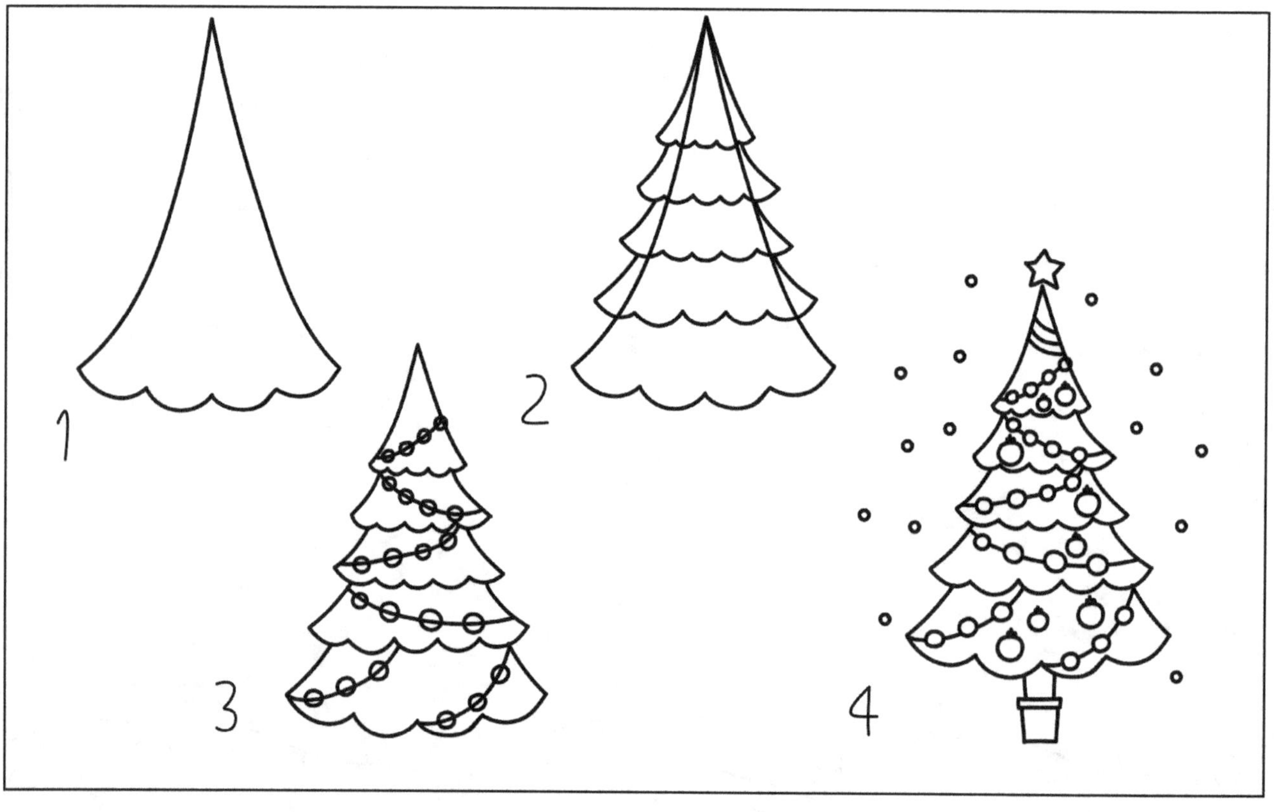

1

2

3

4

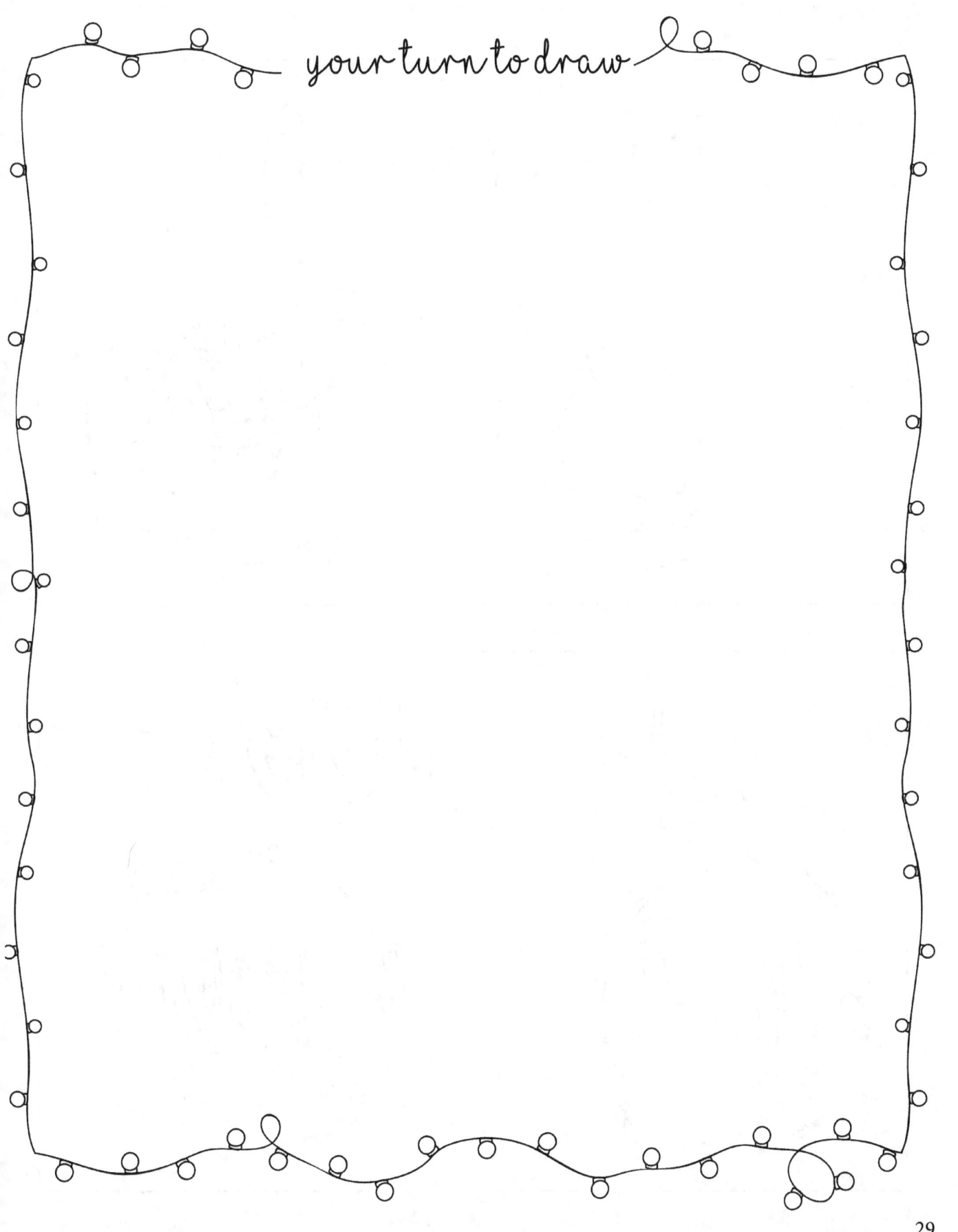

your turn to draw

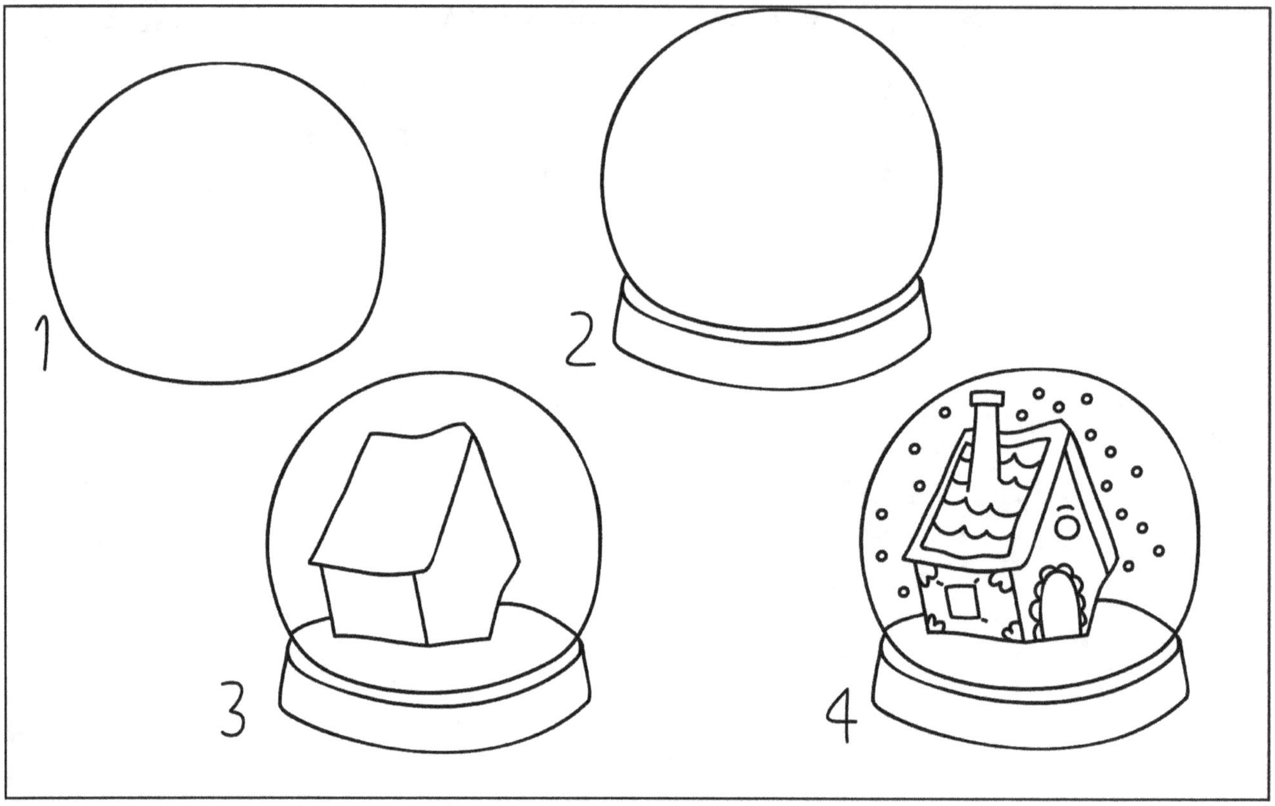

1

2

3

4

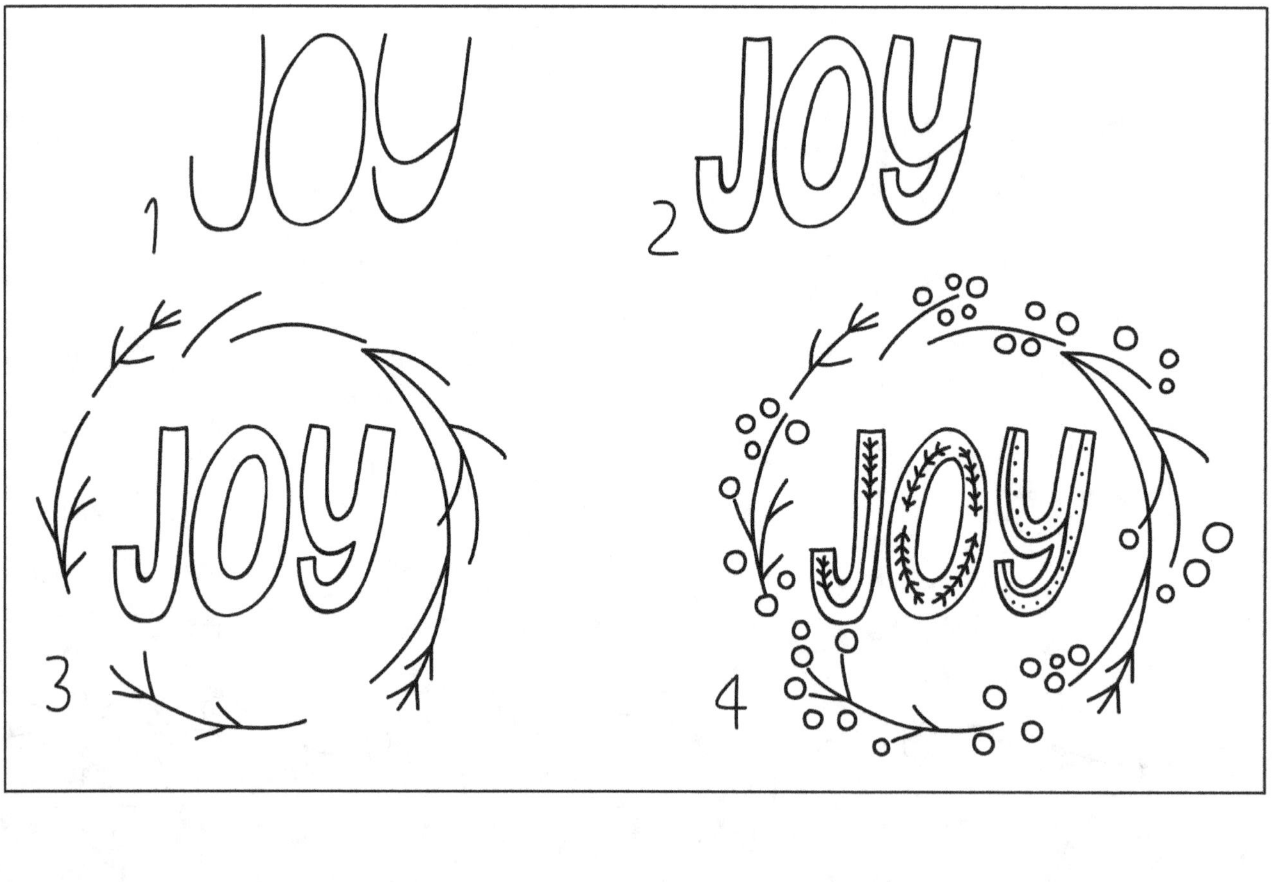

1

2

3

4

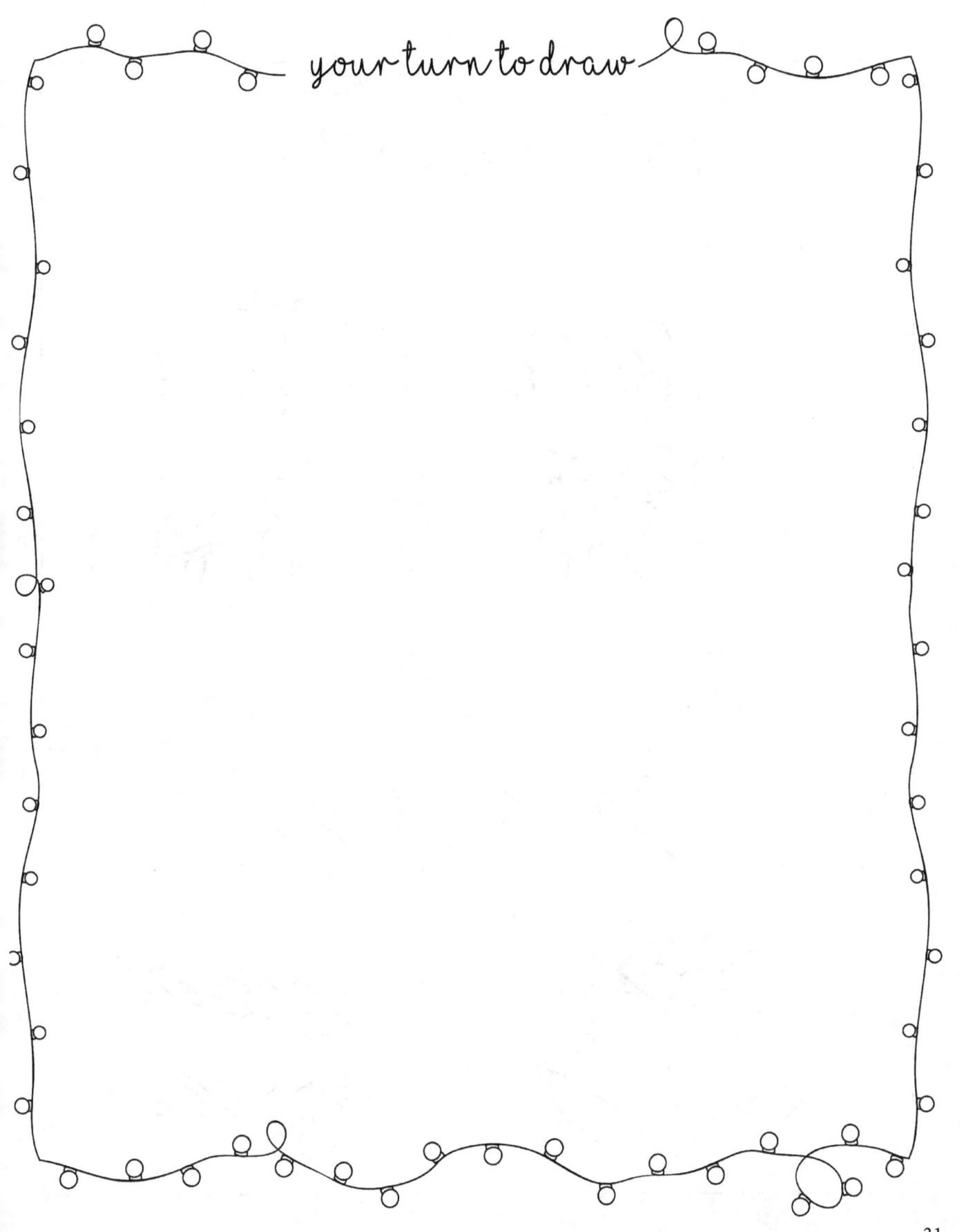

your turn to draw

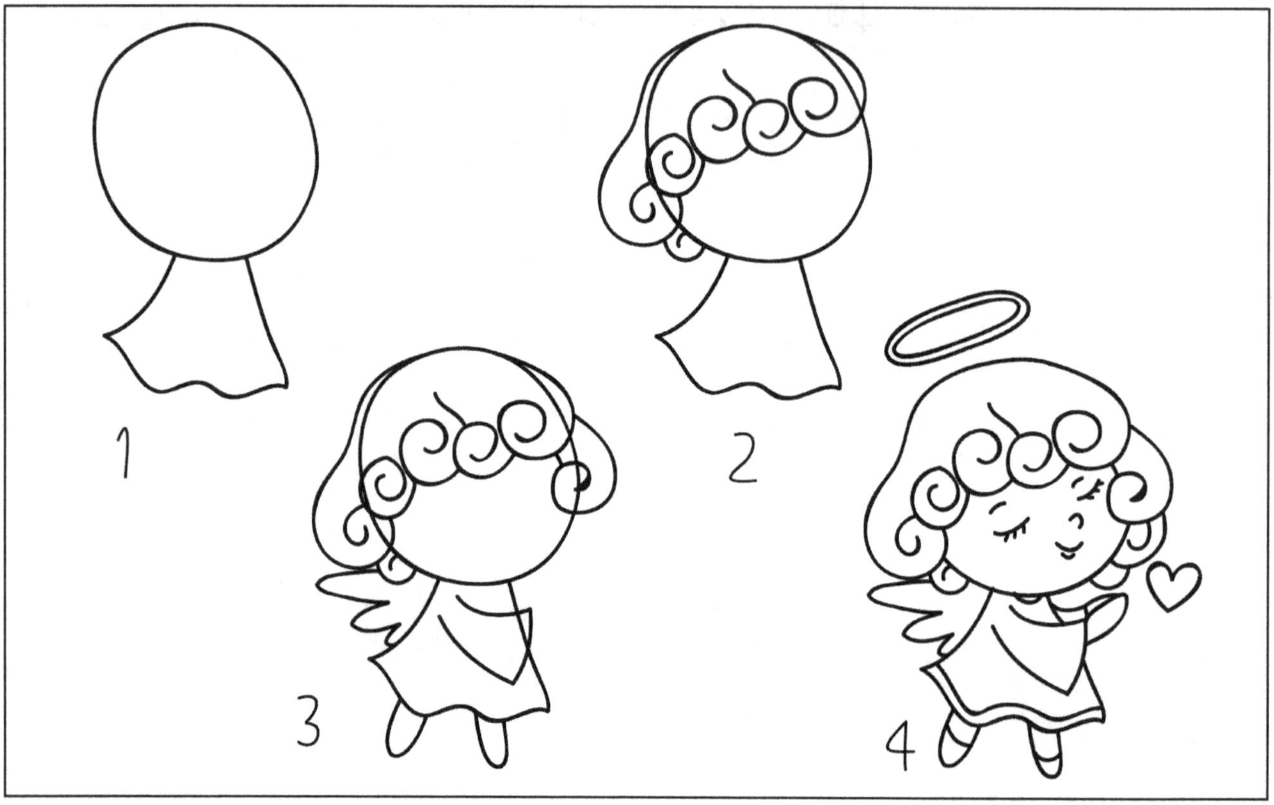

1

2

3

4

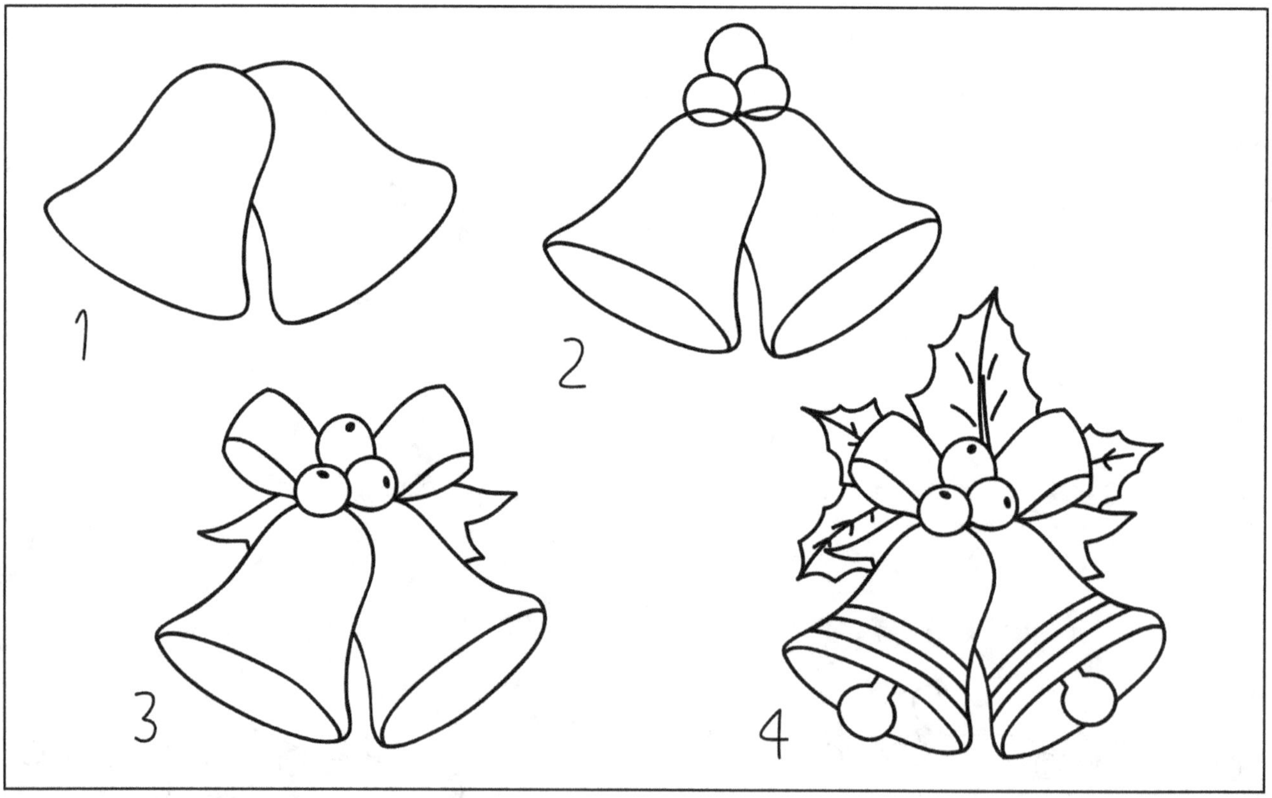

1

2

3

4

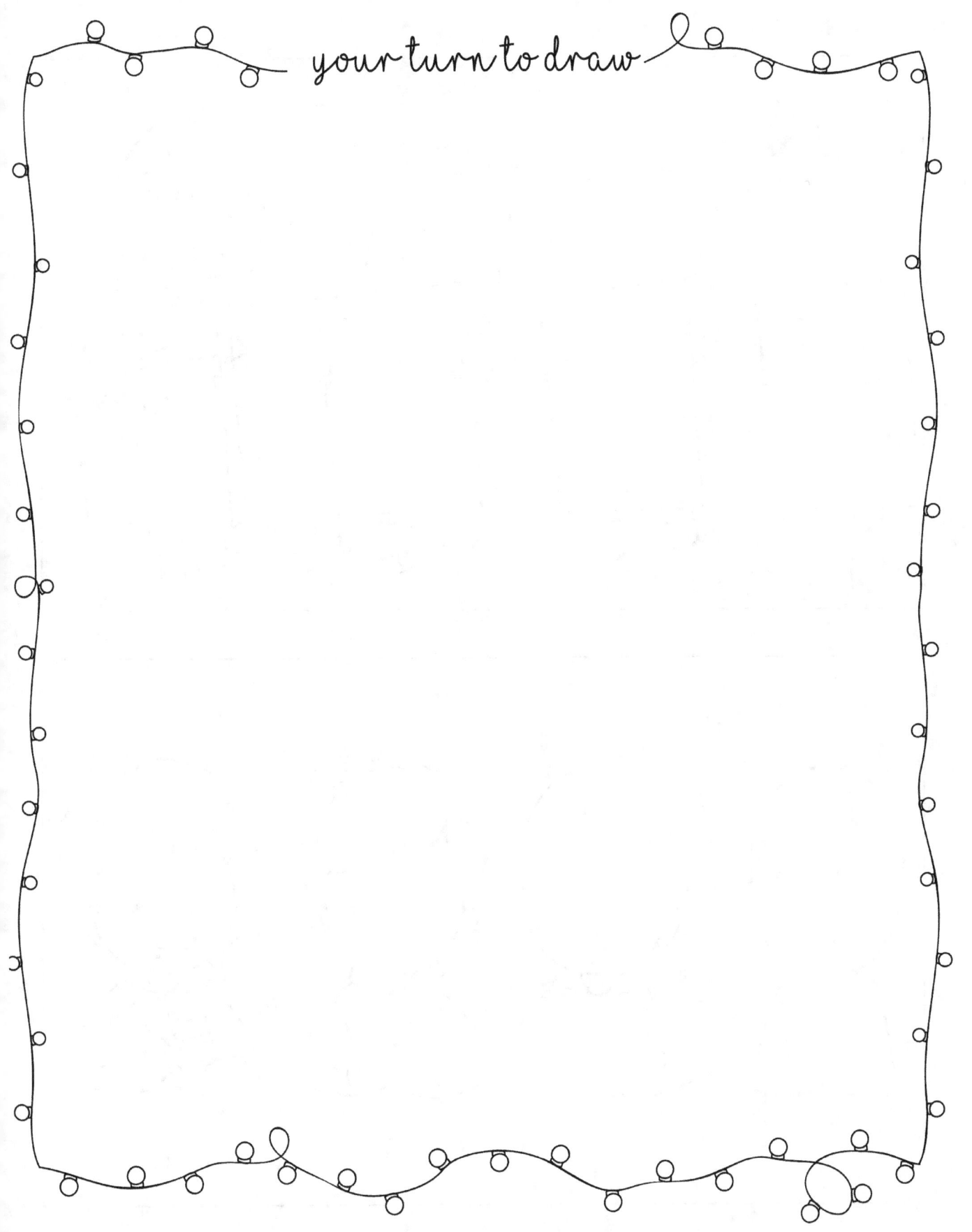

your turn to draw

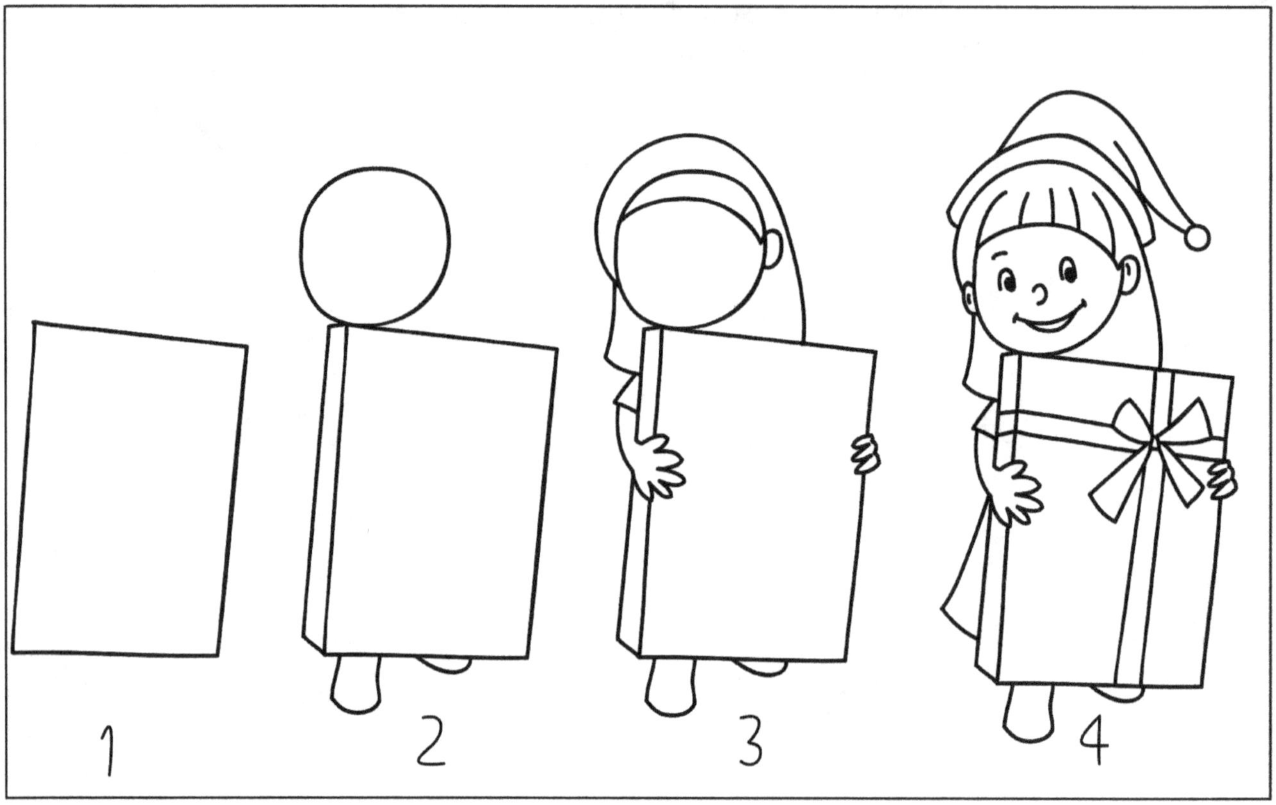

1 2 3 4

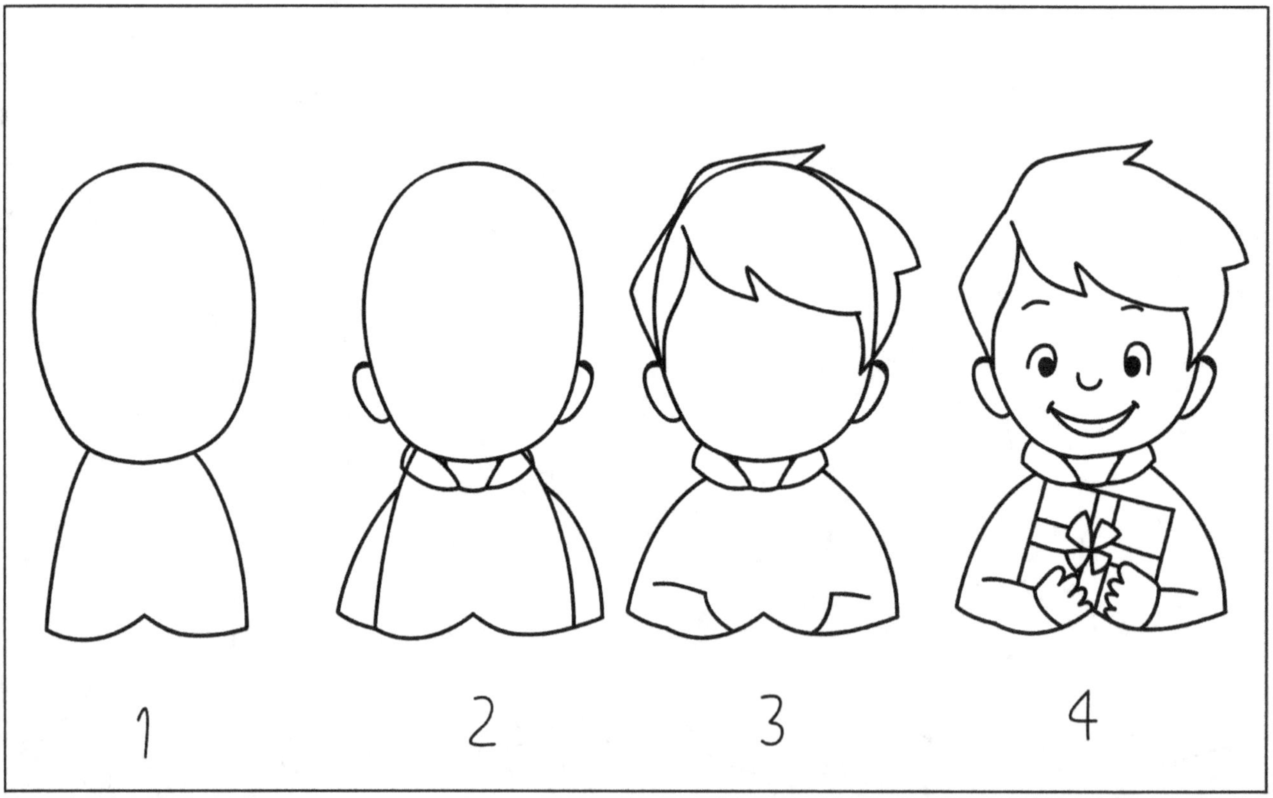

1 2 3 4

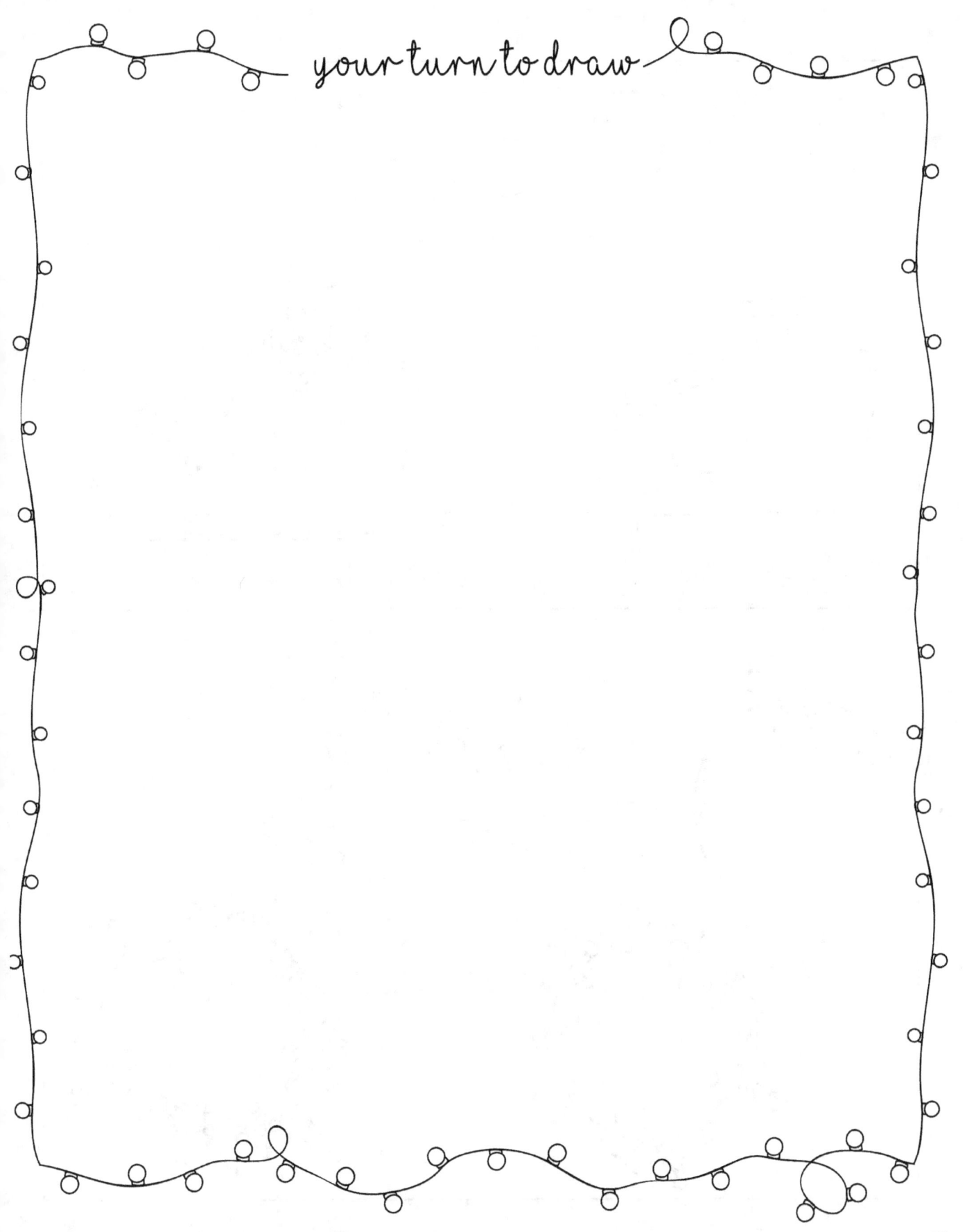

your turn to draw

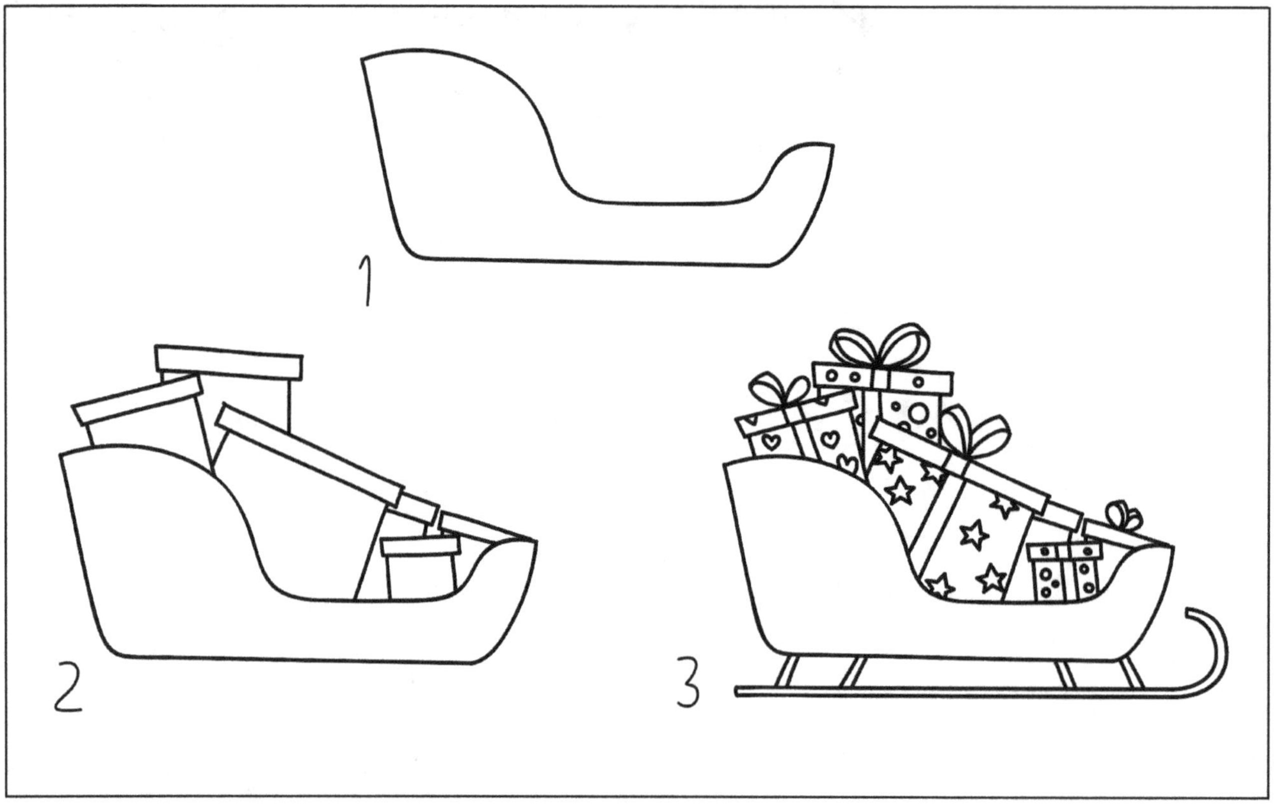

1

2

3

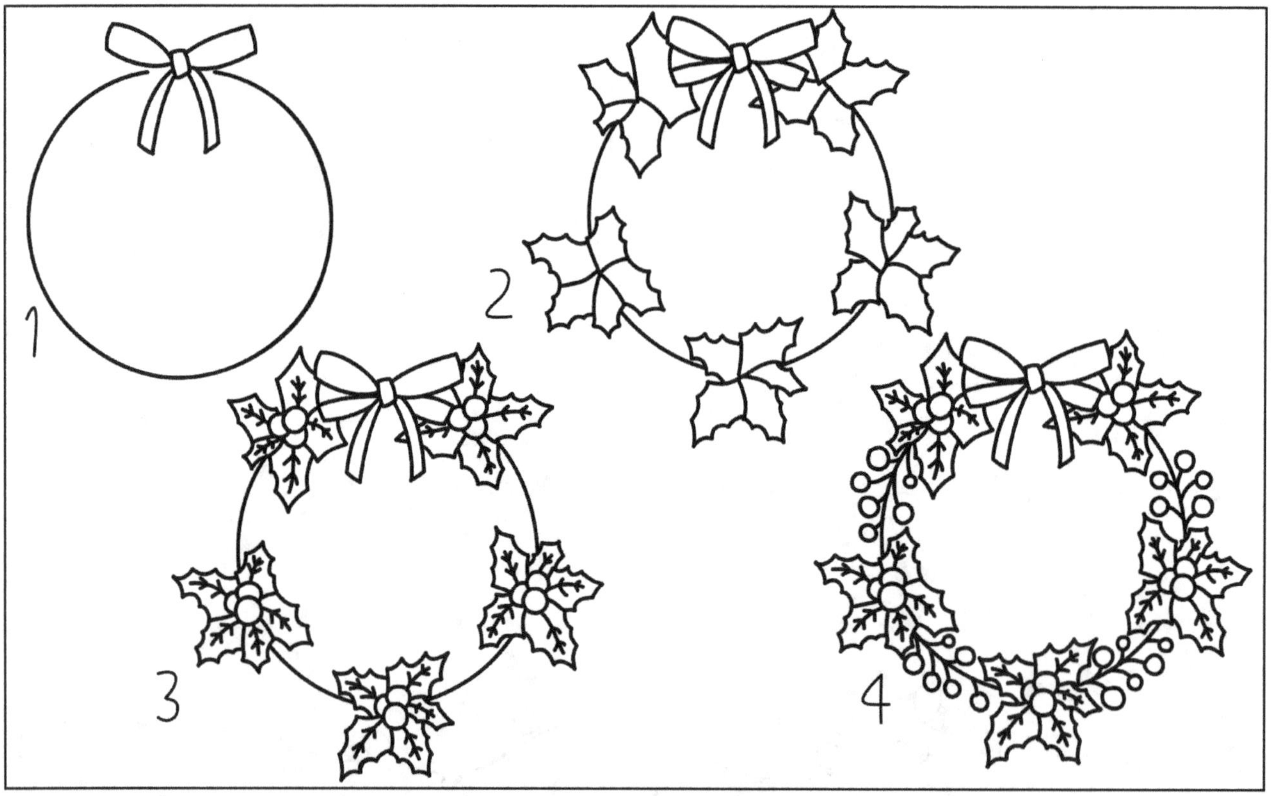

1

2

3

4

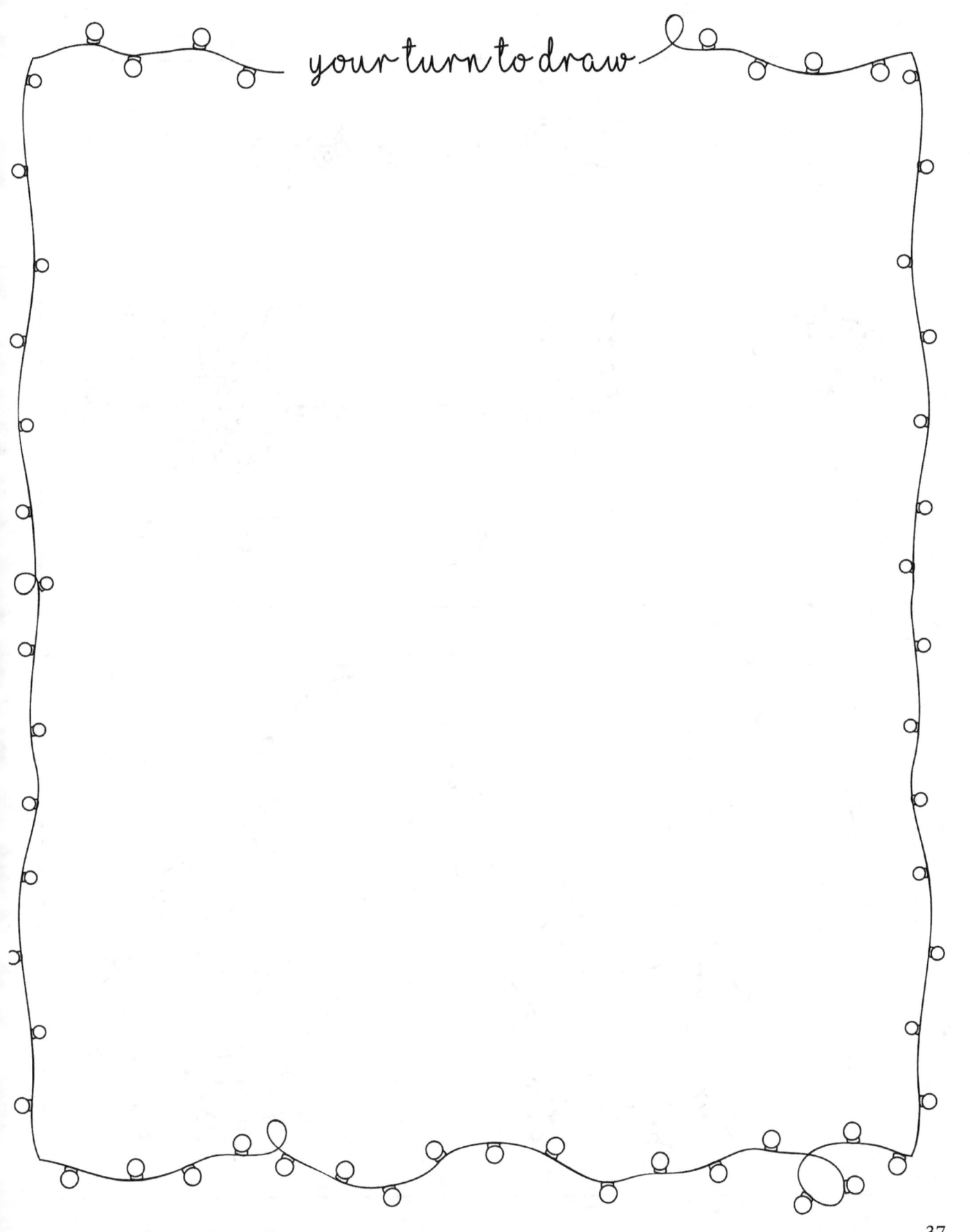

your turn to draw

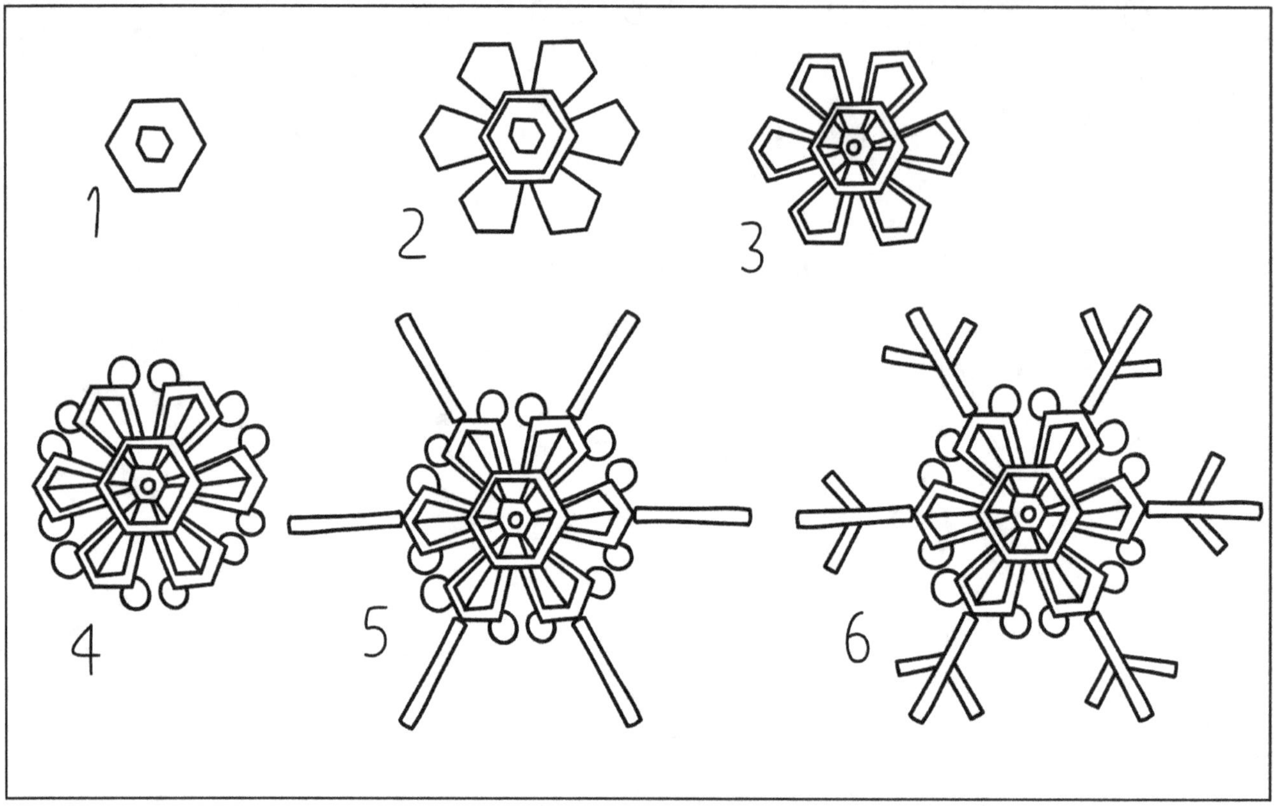

1   2   3   4   5   6

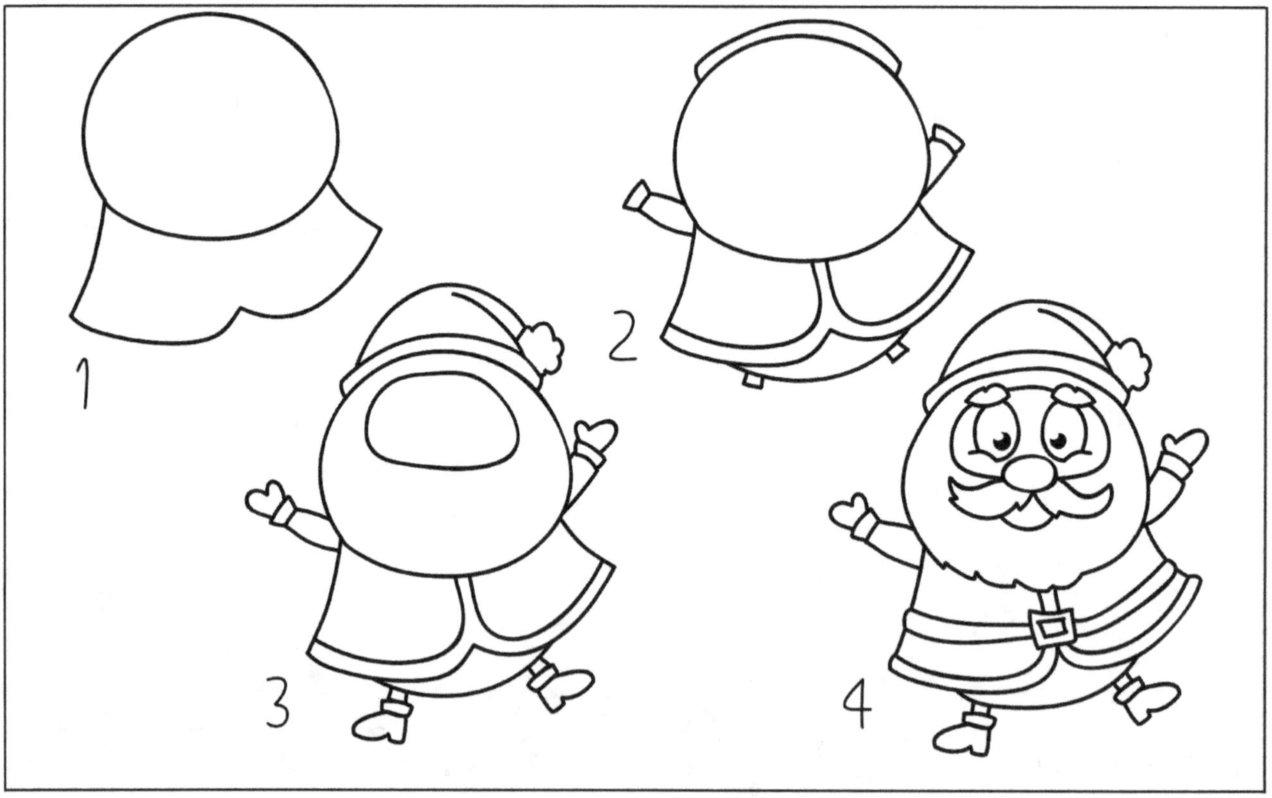

1   2   3   4

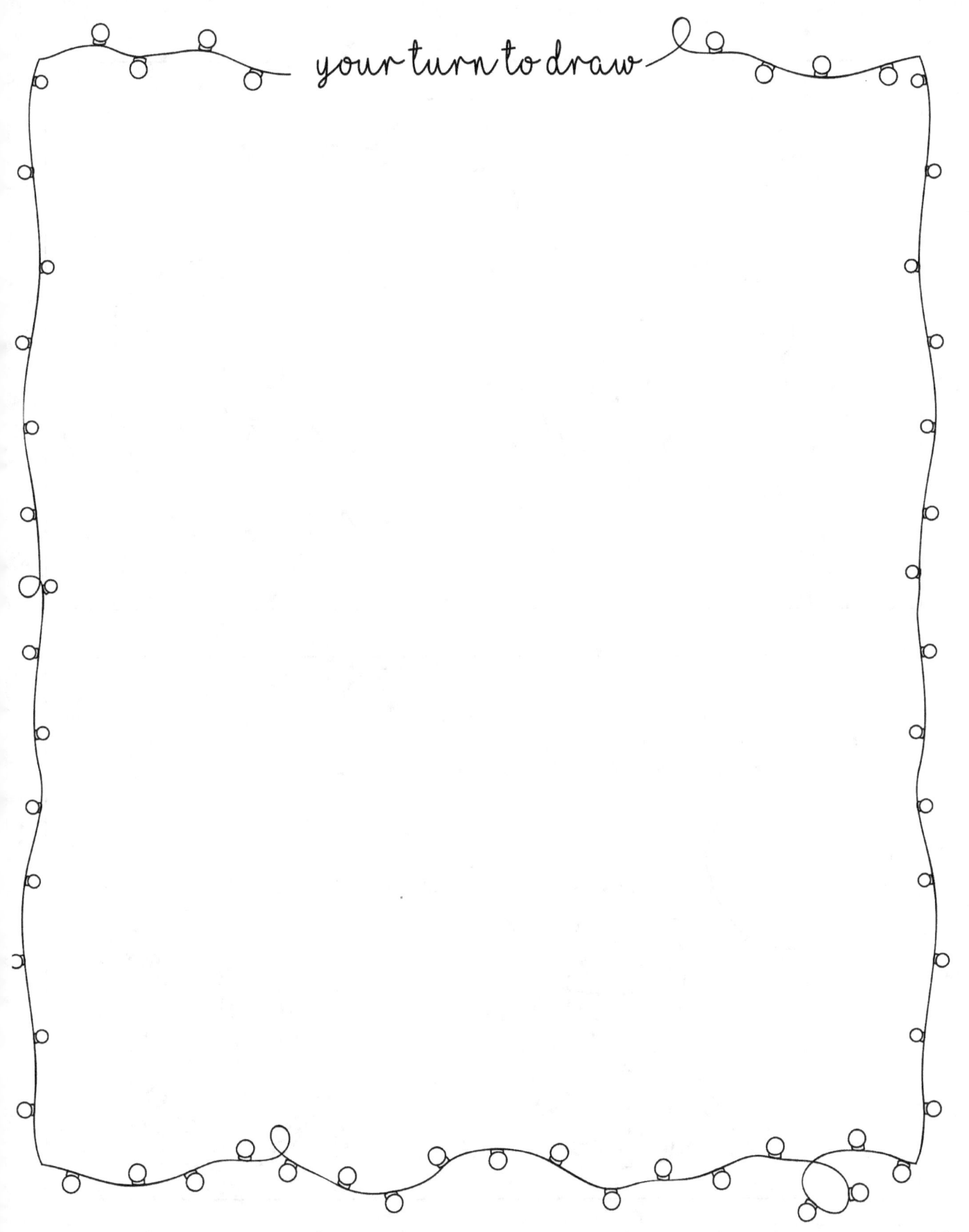

your turn to draw

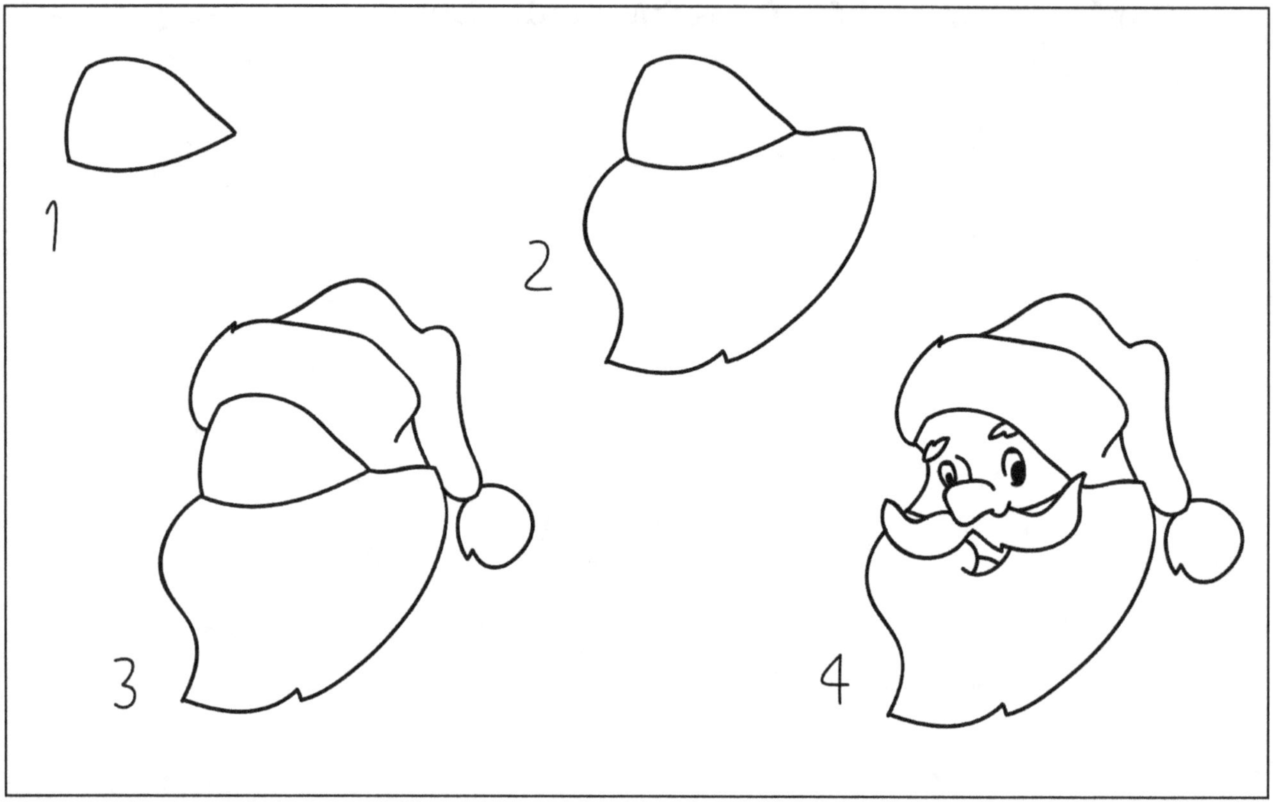

1

2

3

4

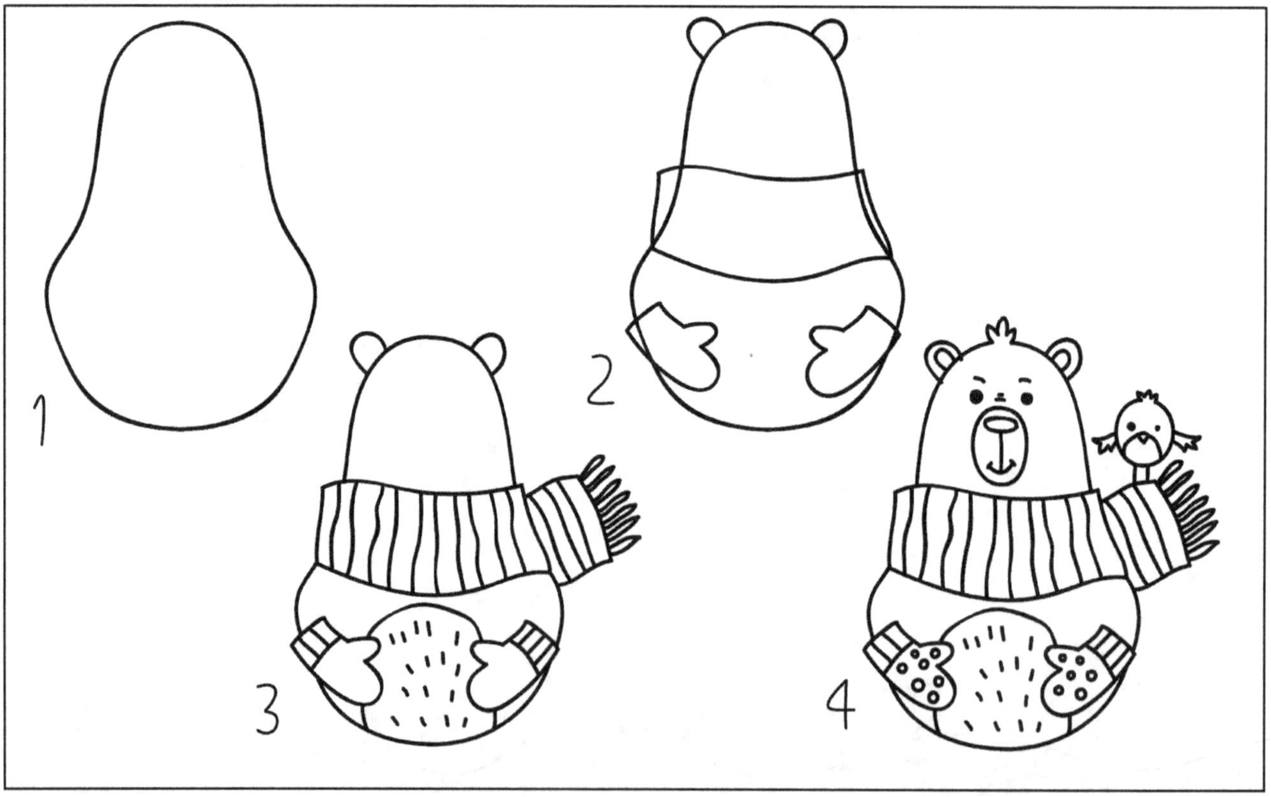

1

2

3

4

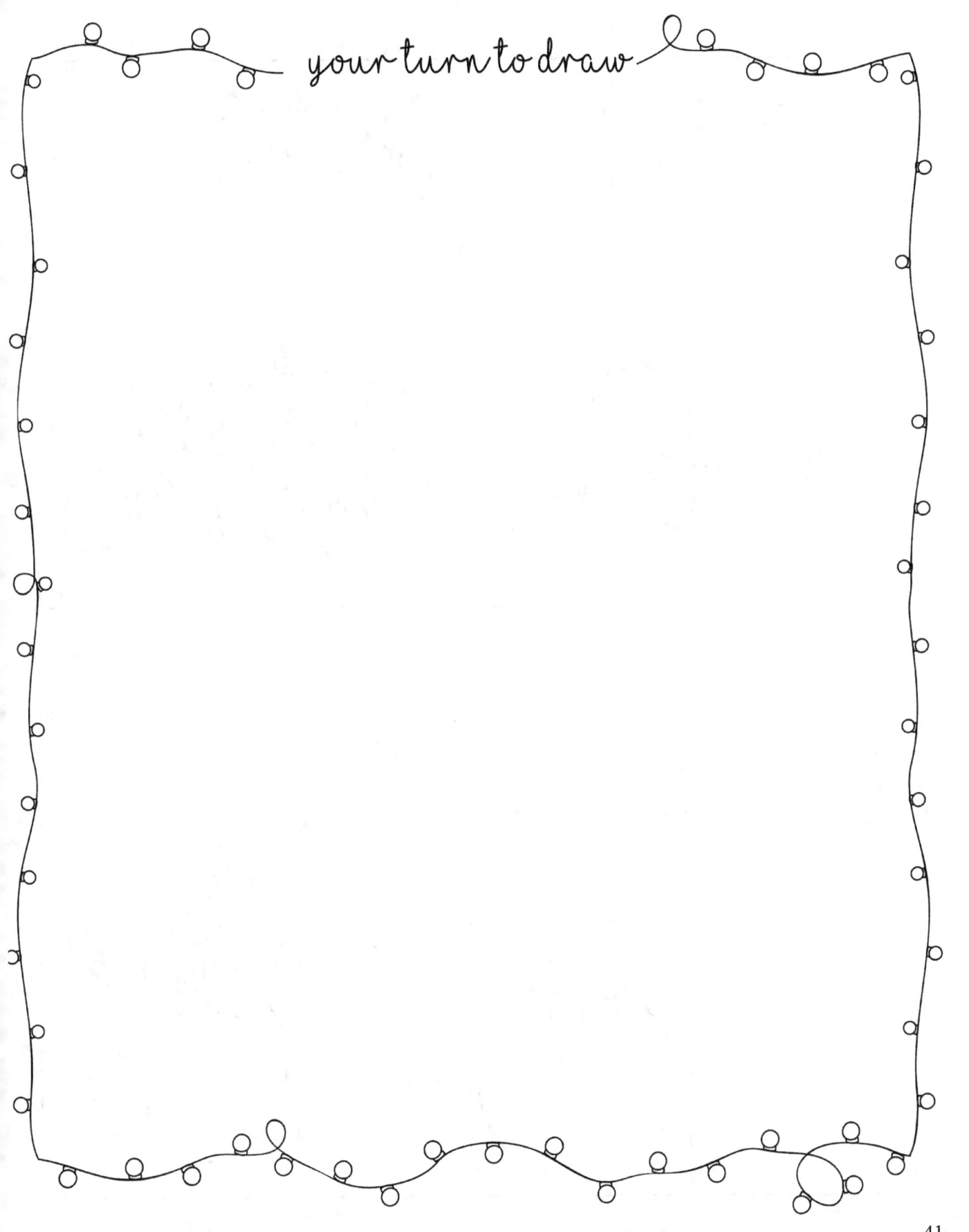

your turn to draw

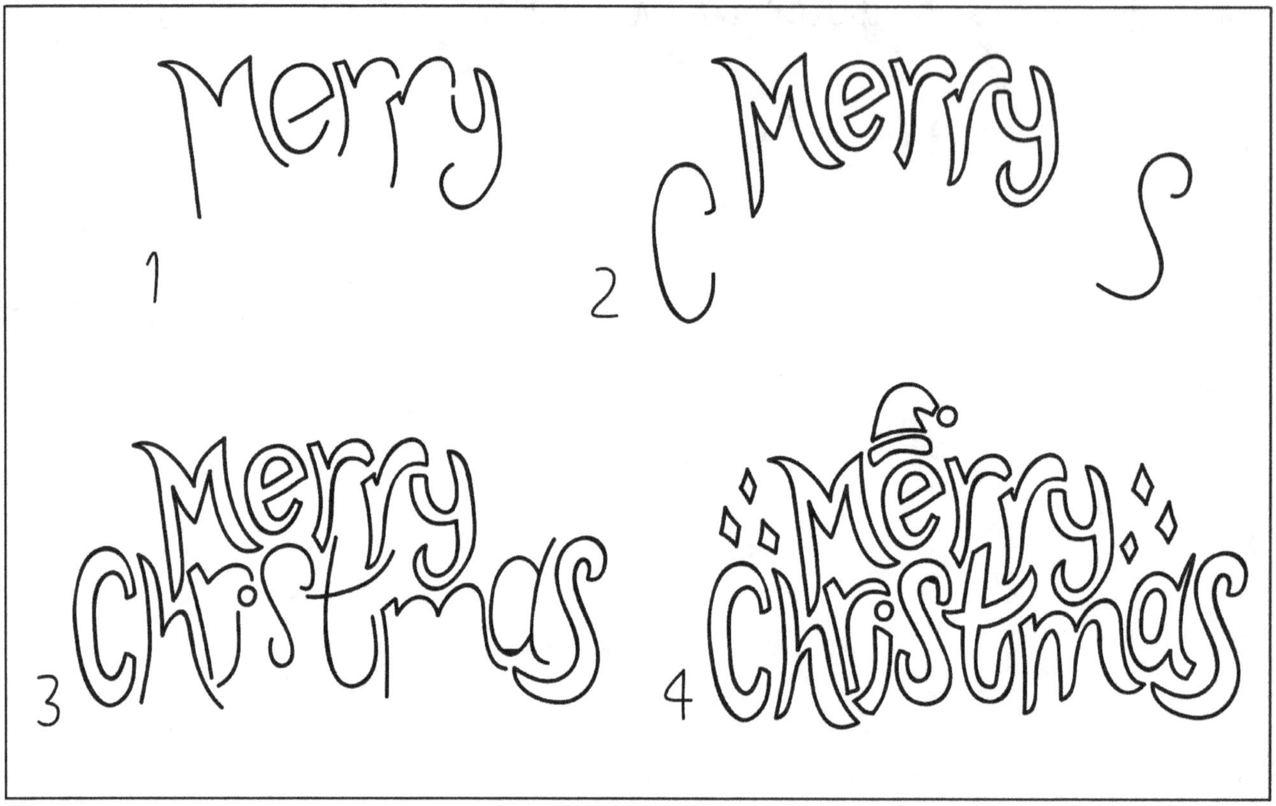

Merry
1

C Merry S
2

Merry
Christmas
3

Merry
Christmas
4

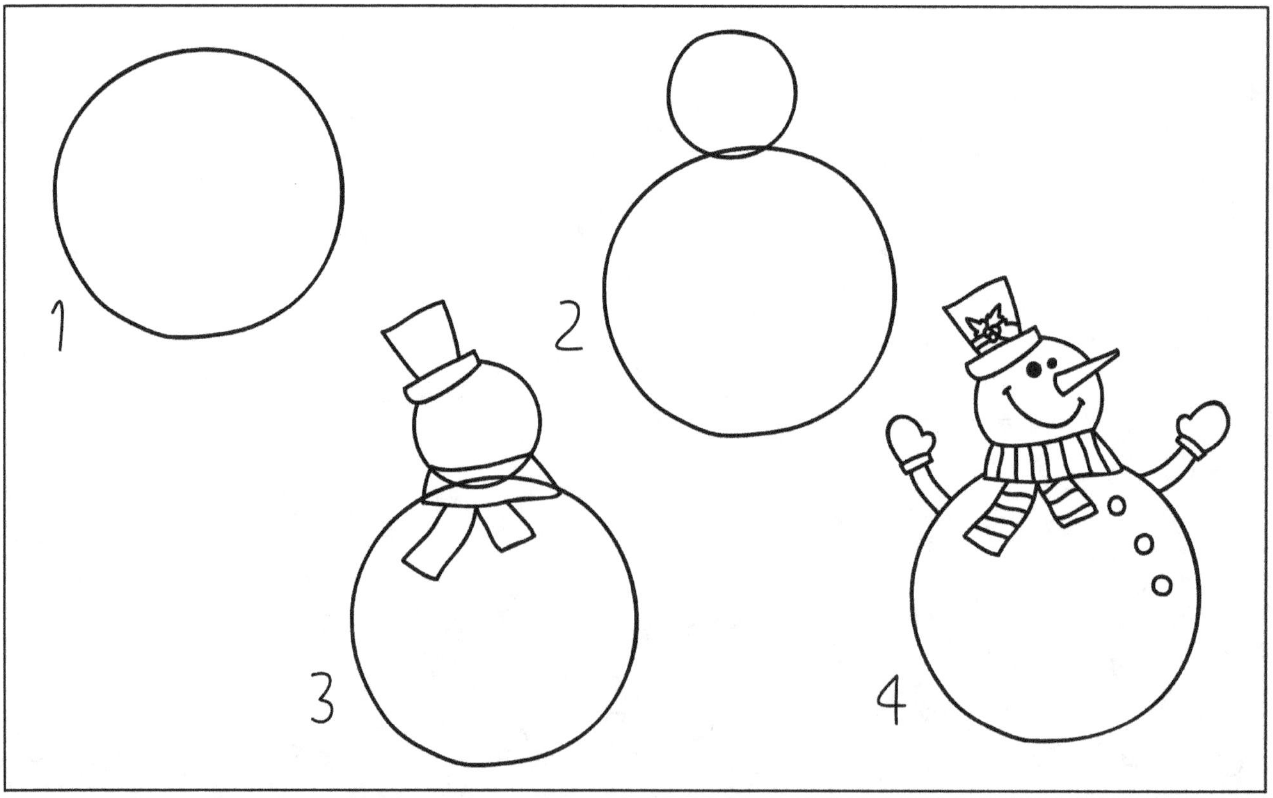

1

2

3

4

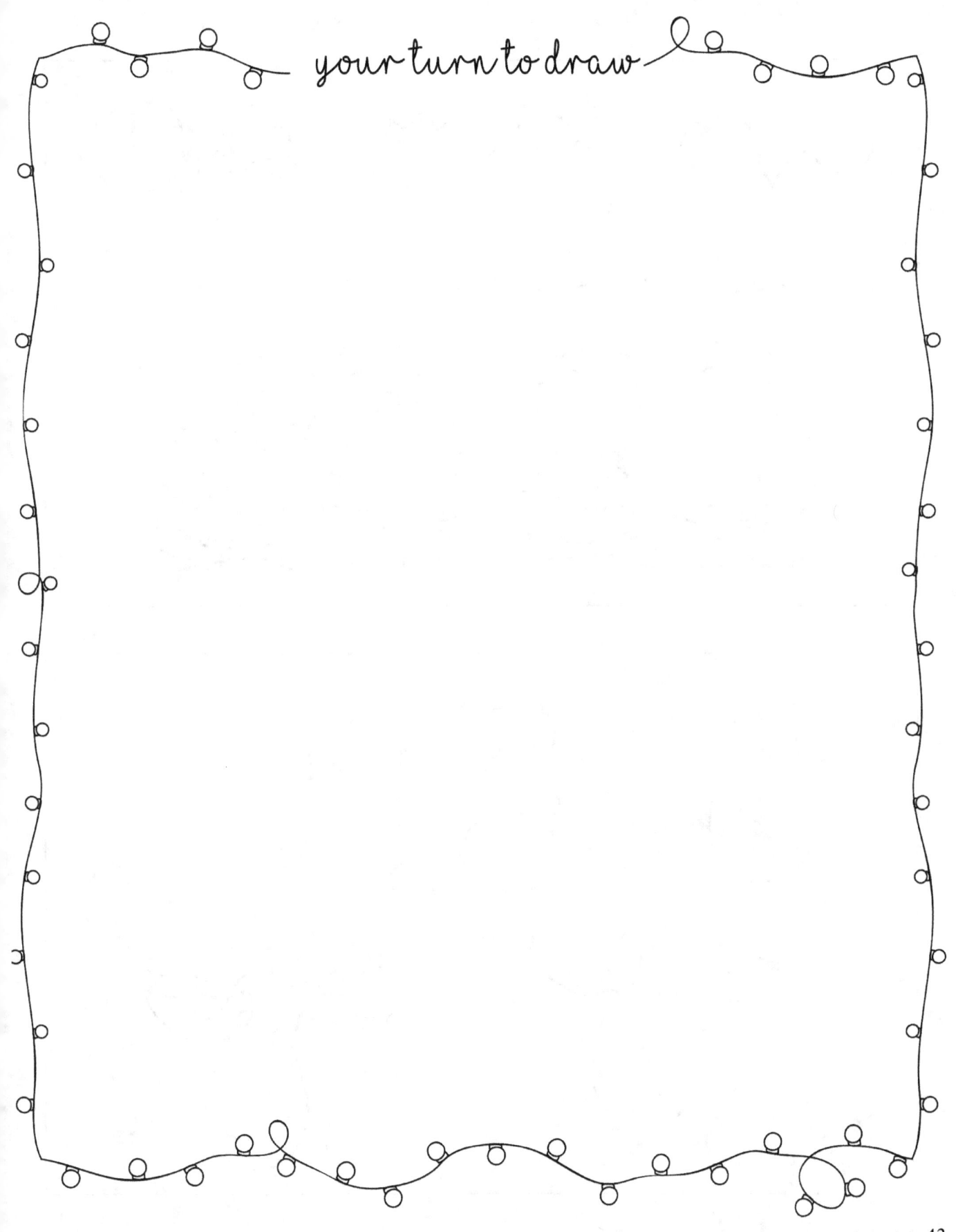

your turn to draw

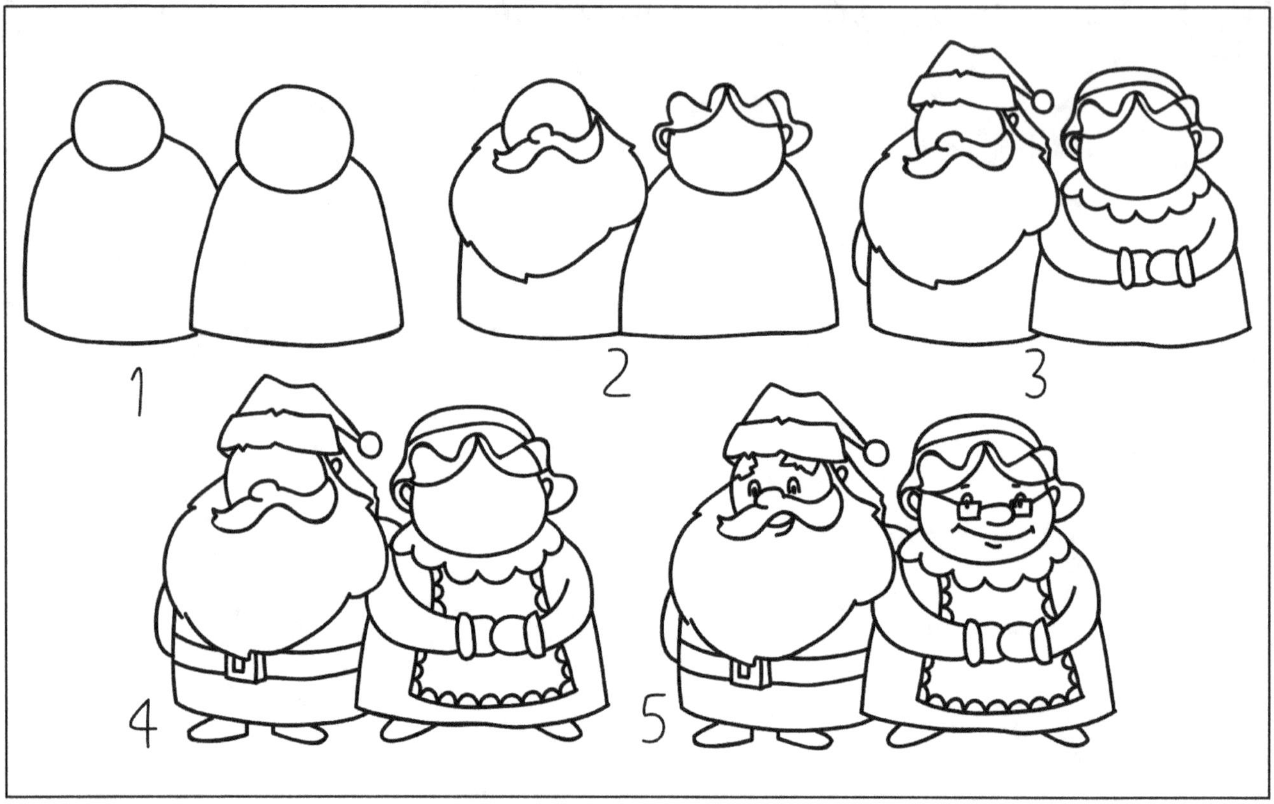

1

2

3

4

5

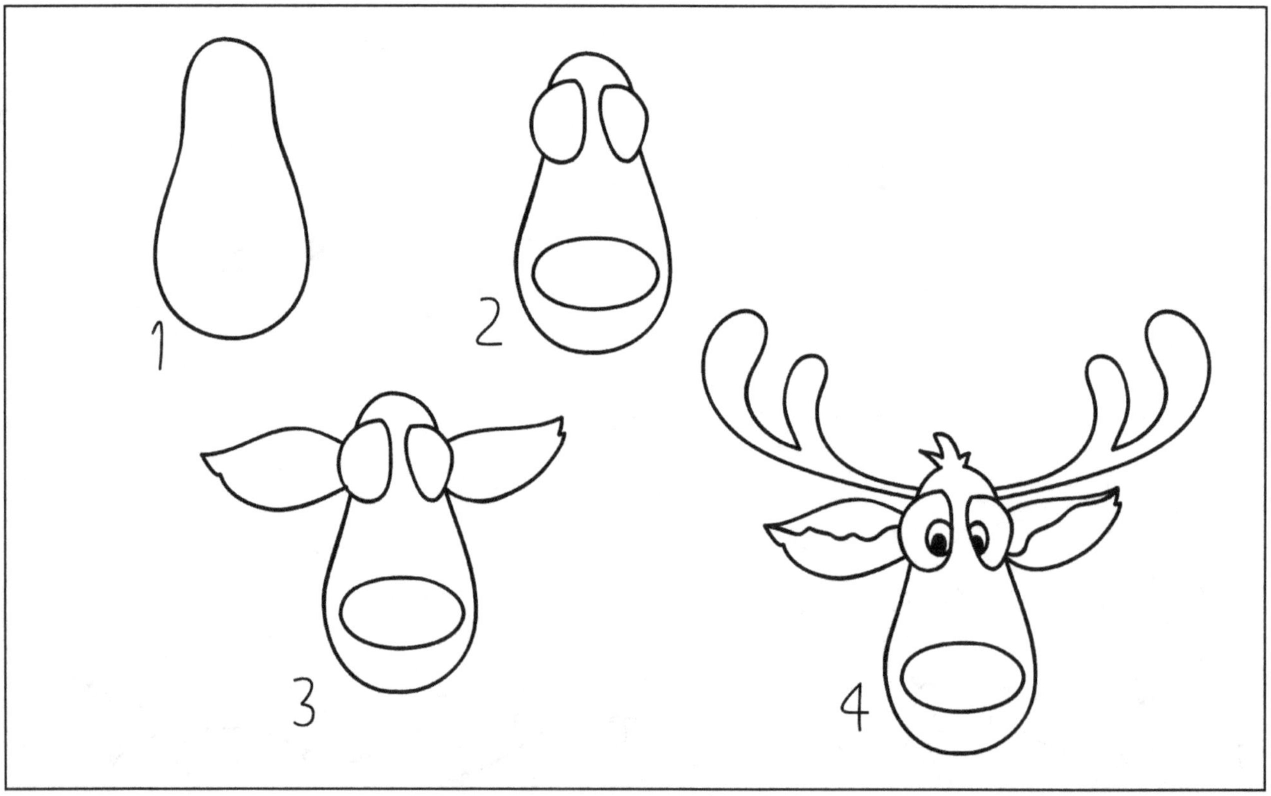

1

2

3

4

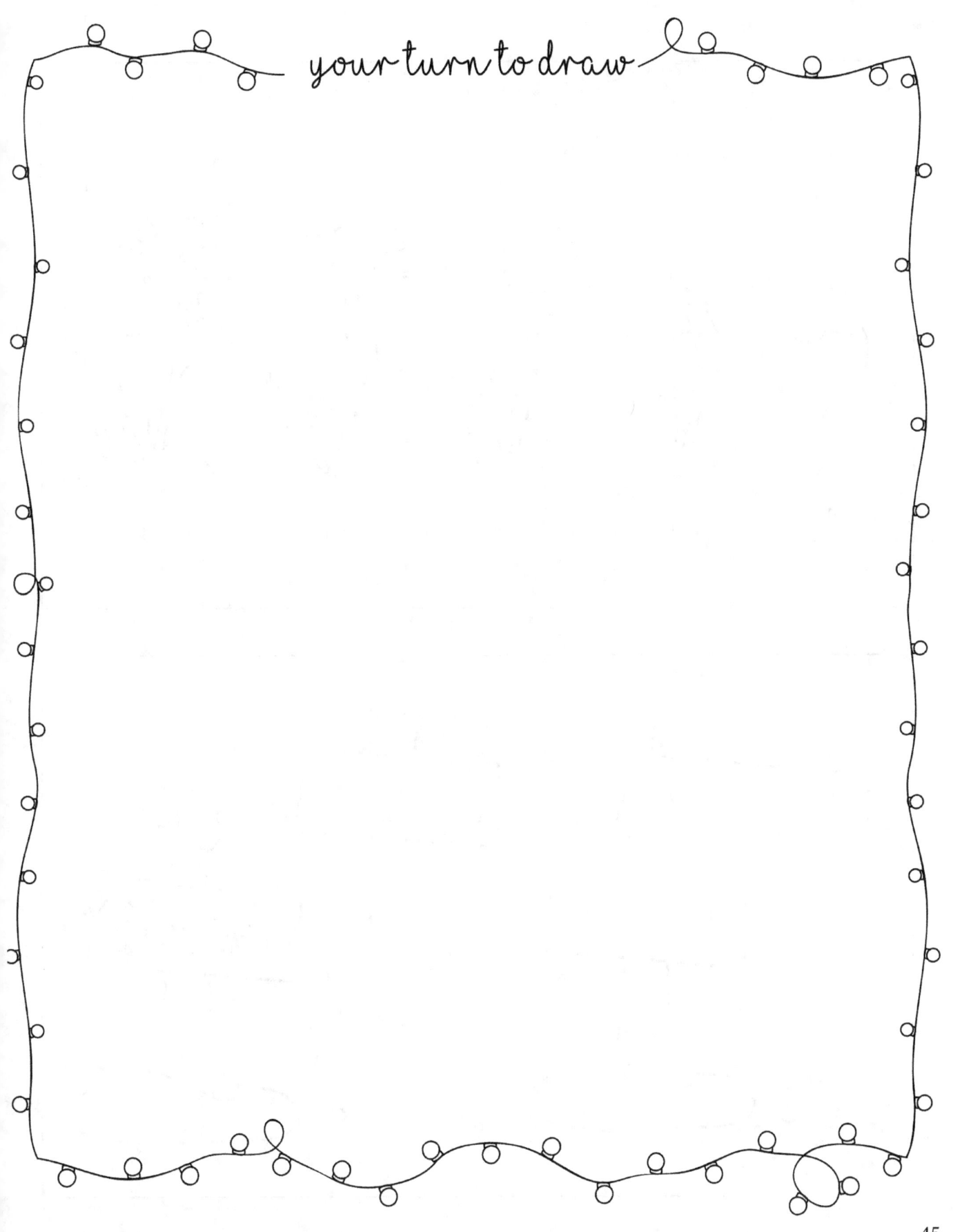

your turn to draw

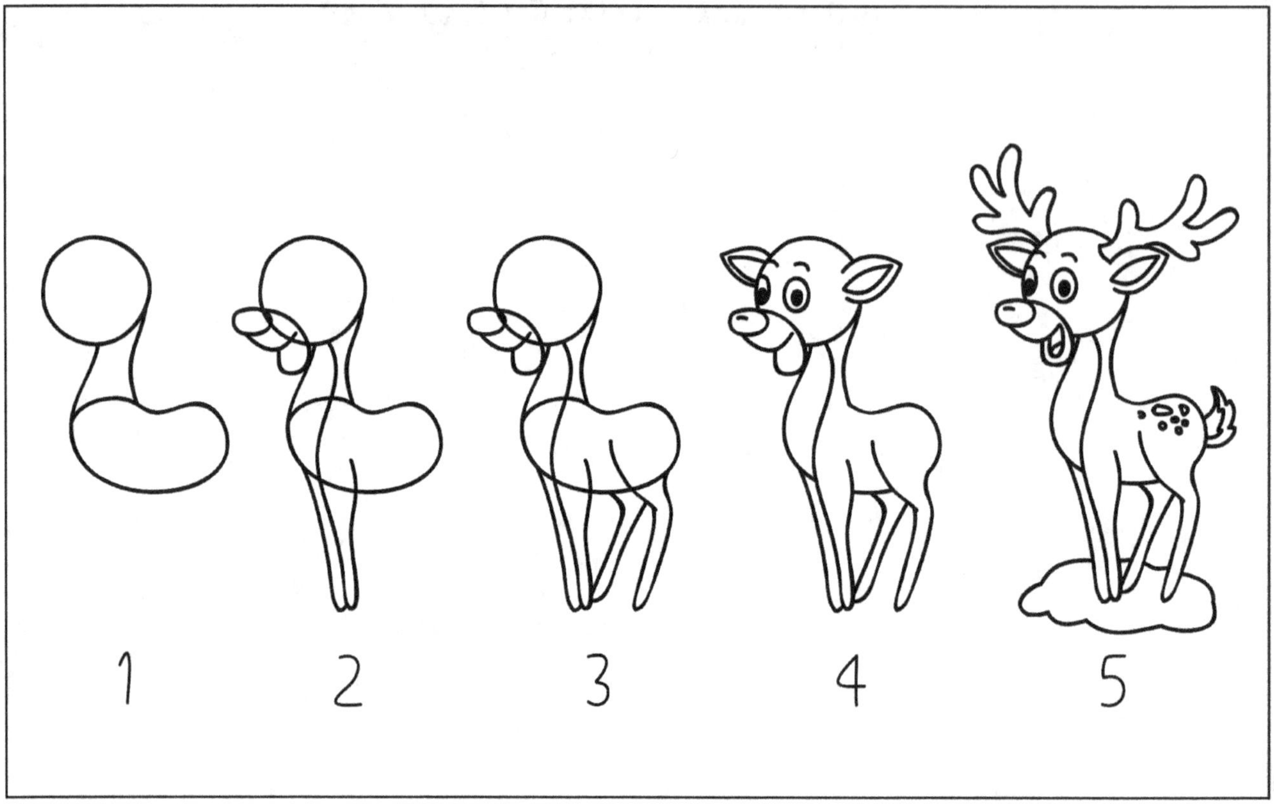

1

2

3

4

5

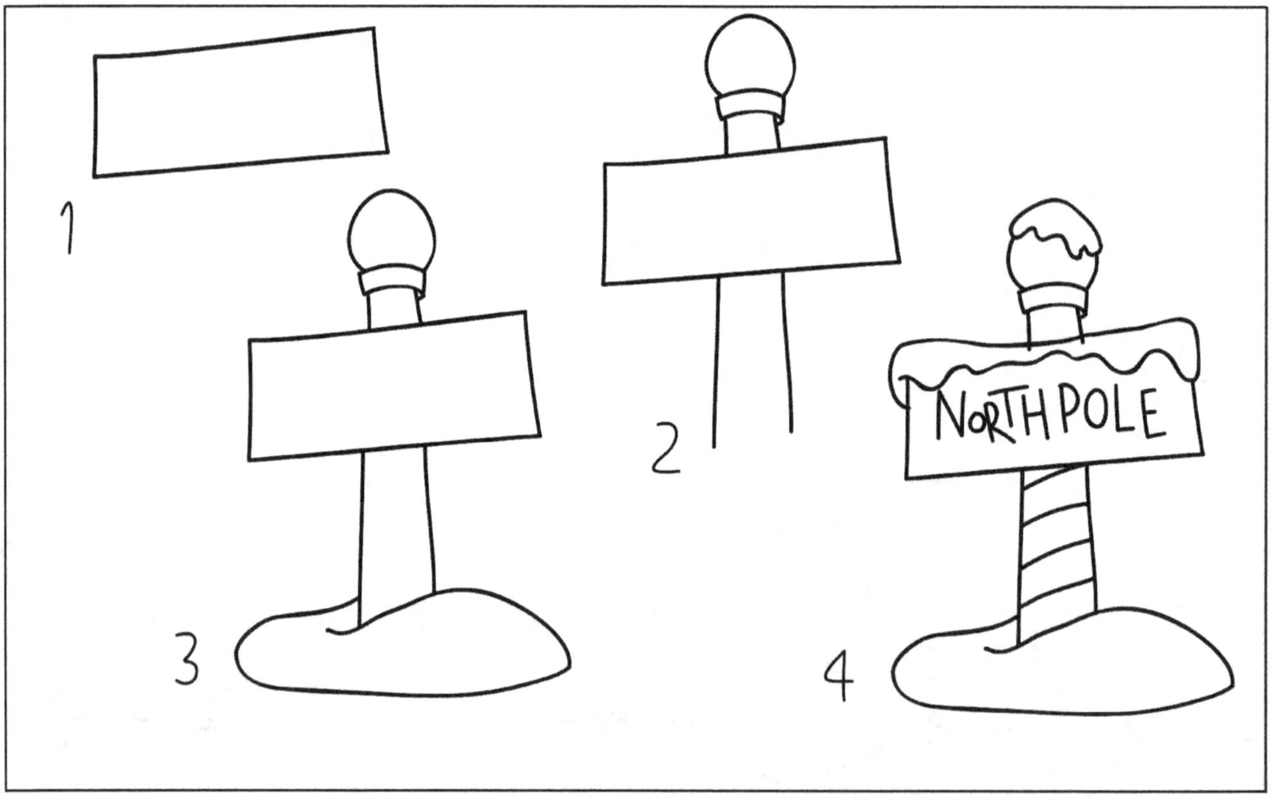

1

2

3

4

NORTH POLE

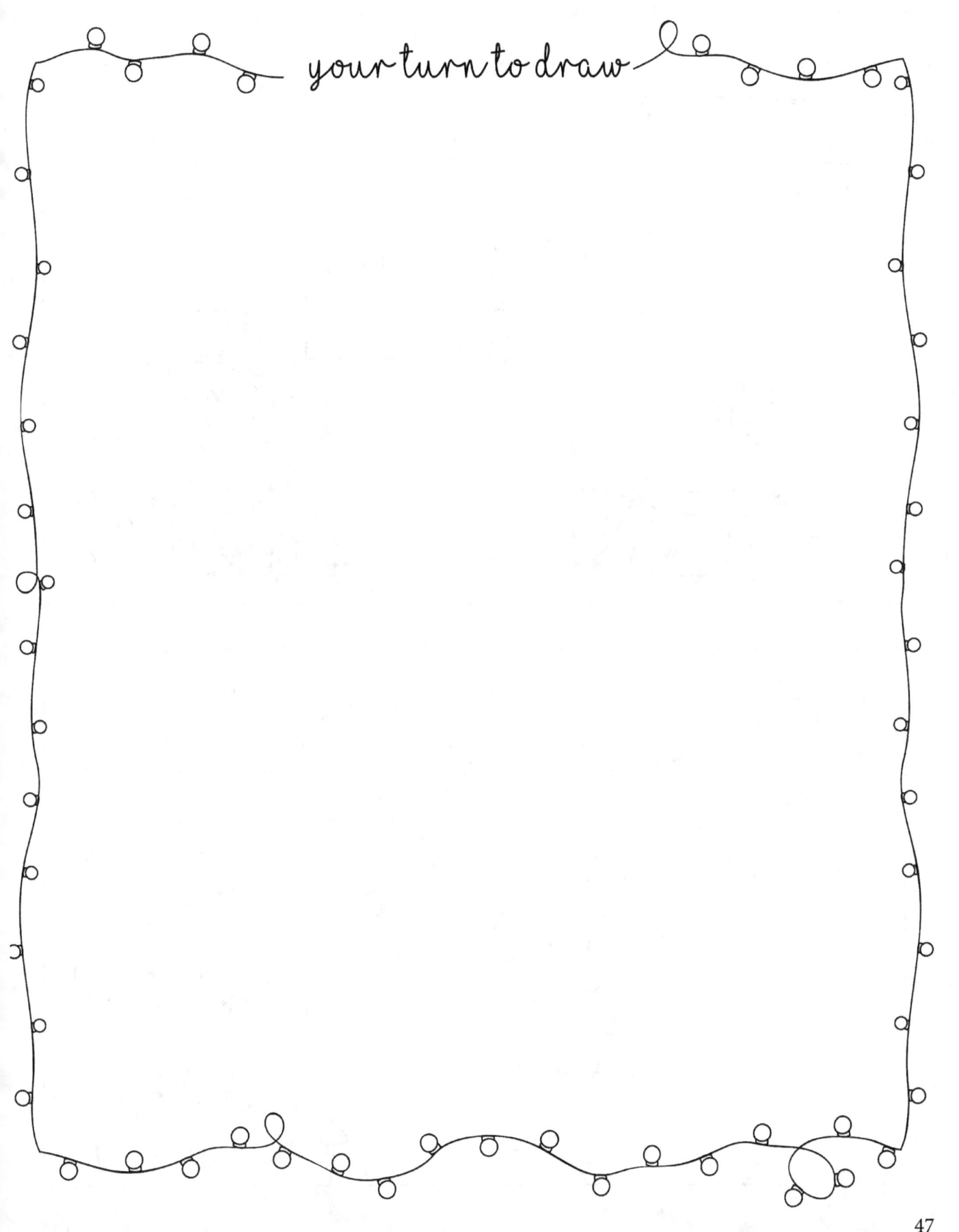

your turn to draw

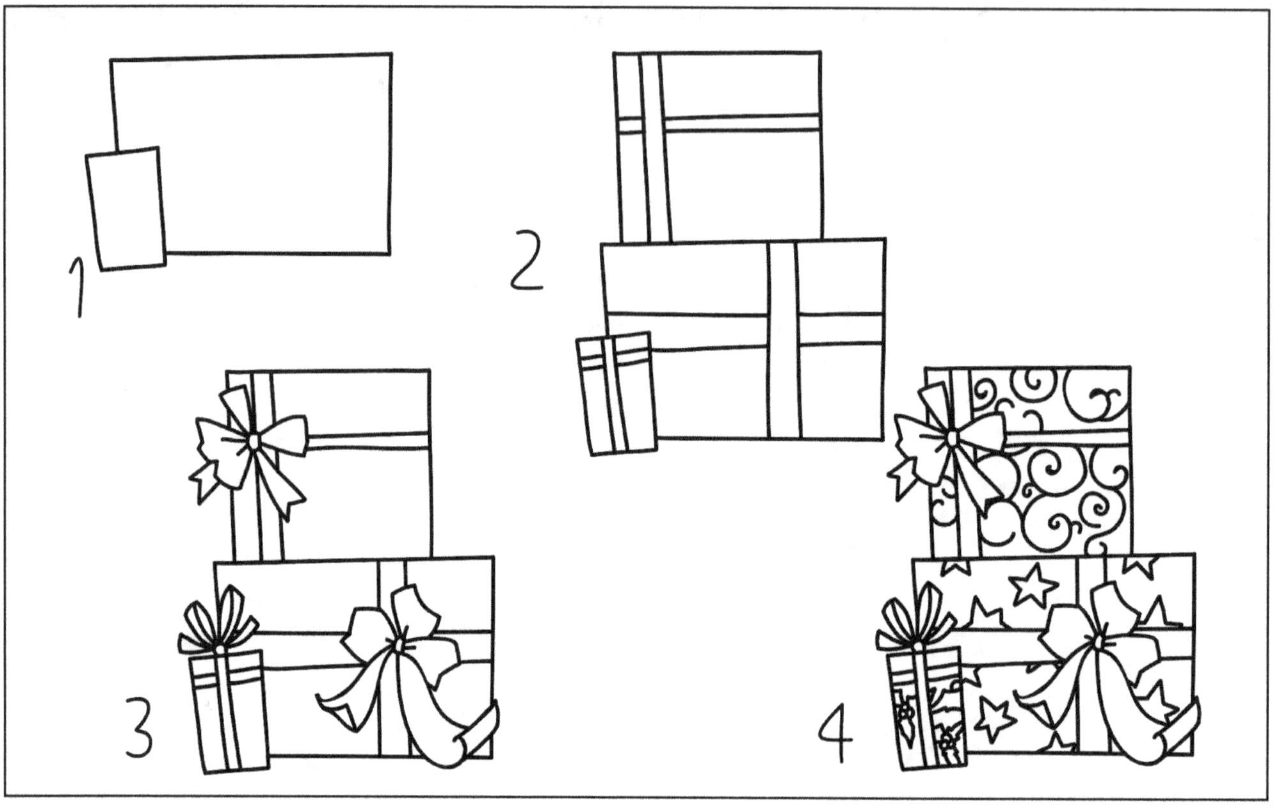

1

2

3

4

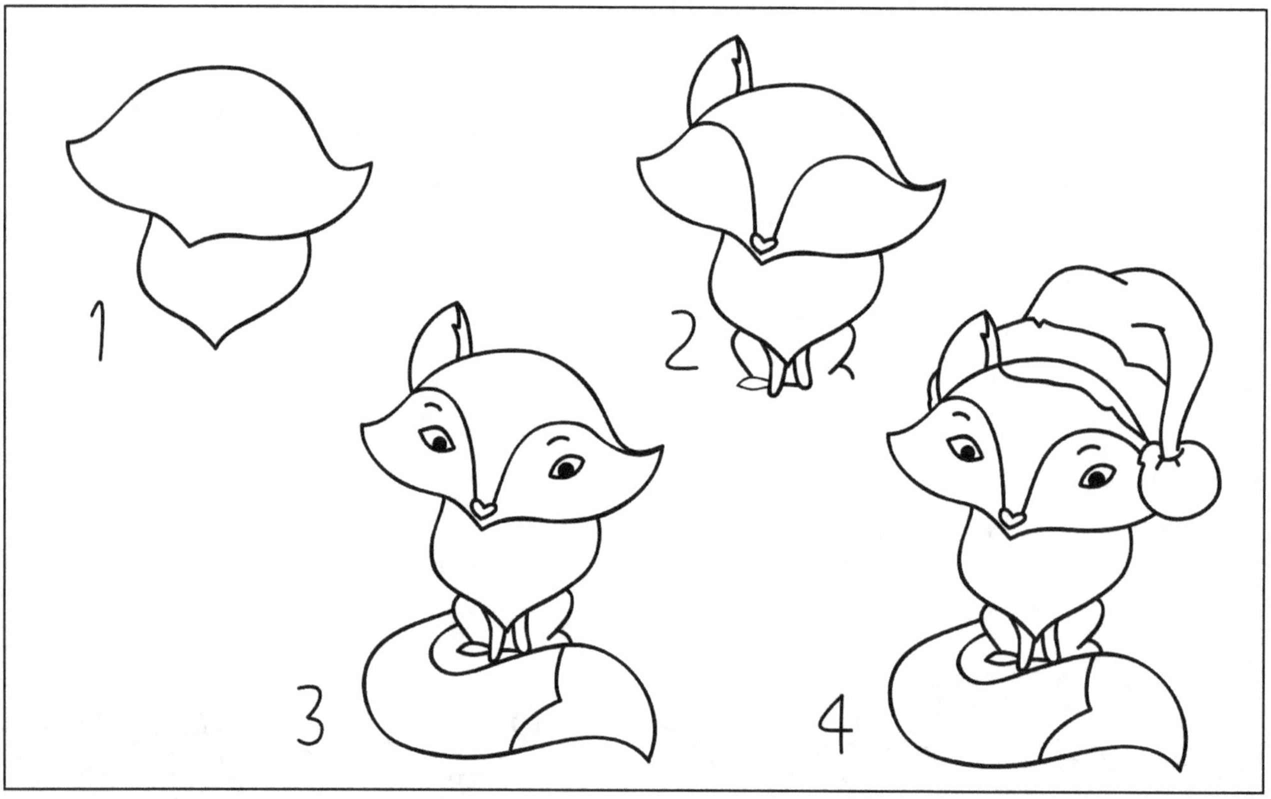

1

2

3

4

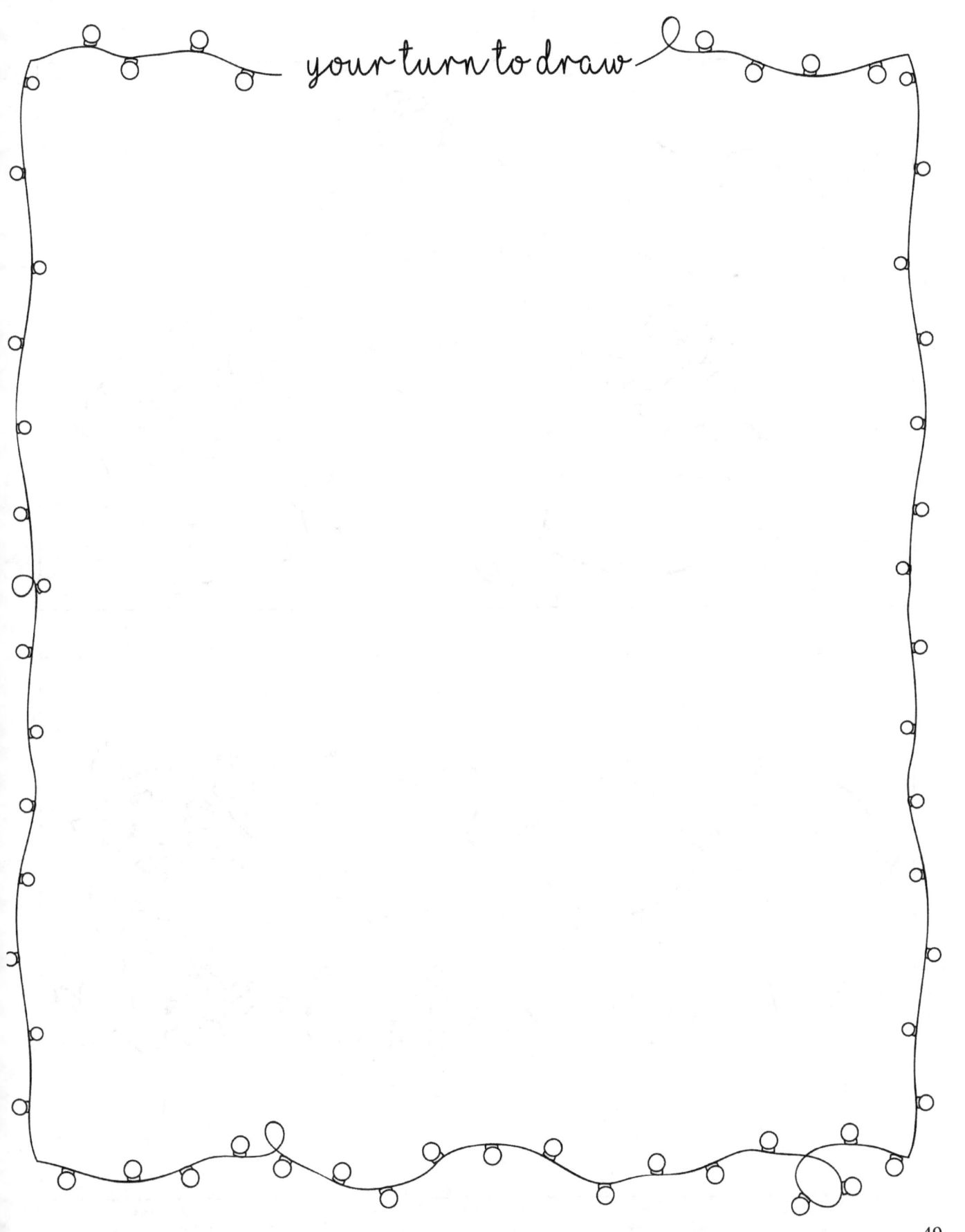

your turn to draw

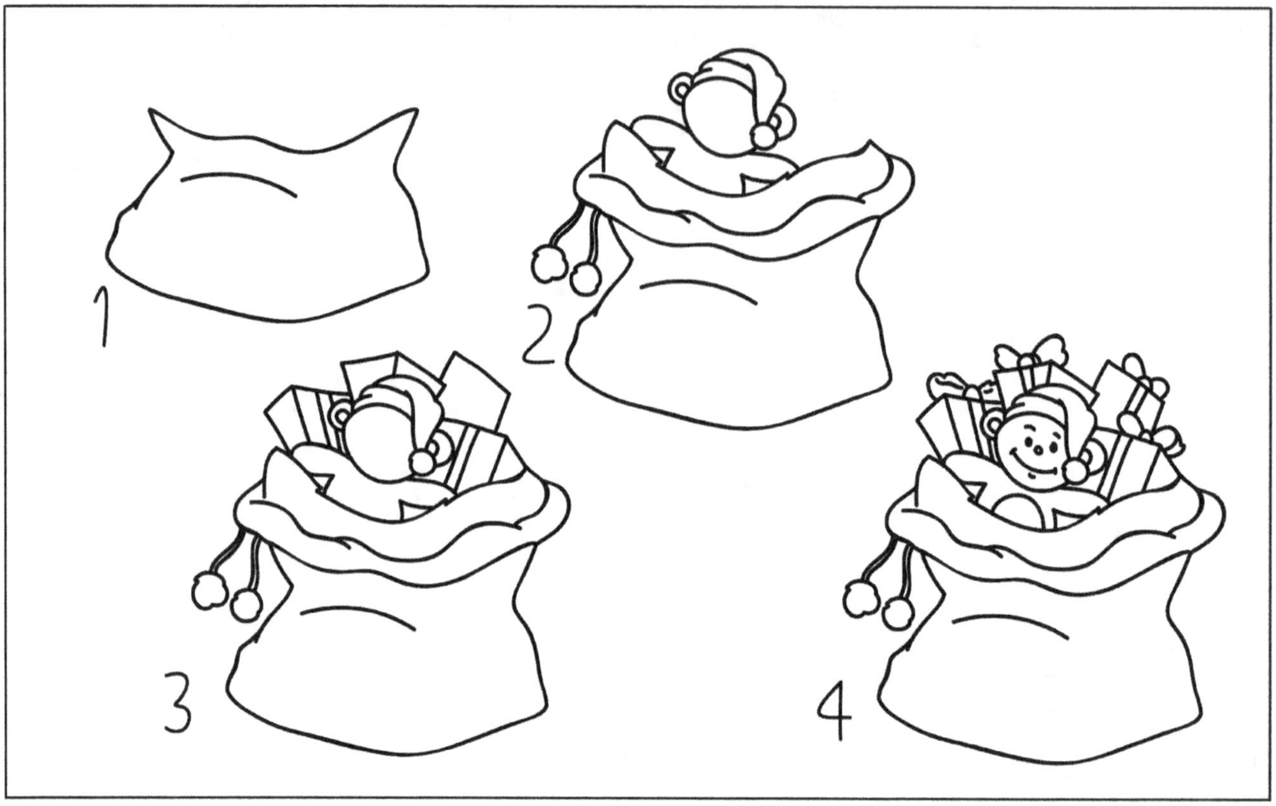

1

2

3

4

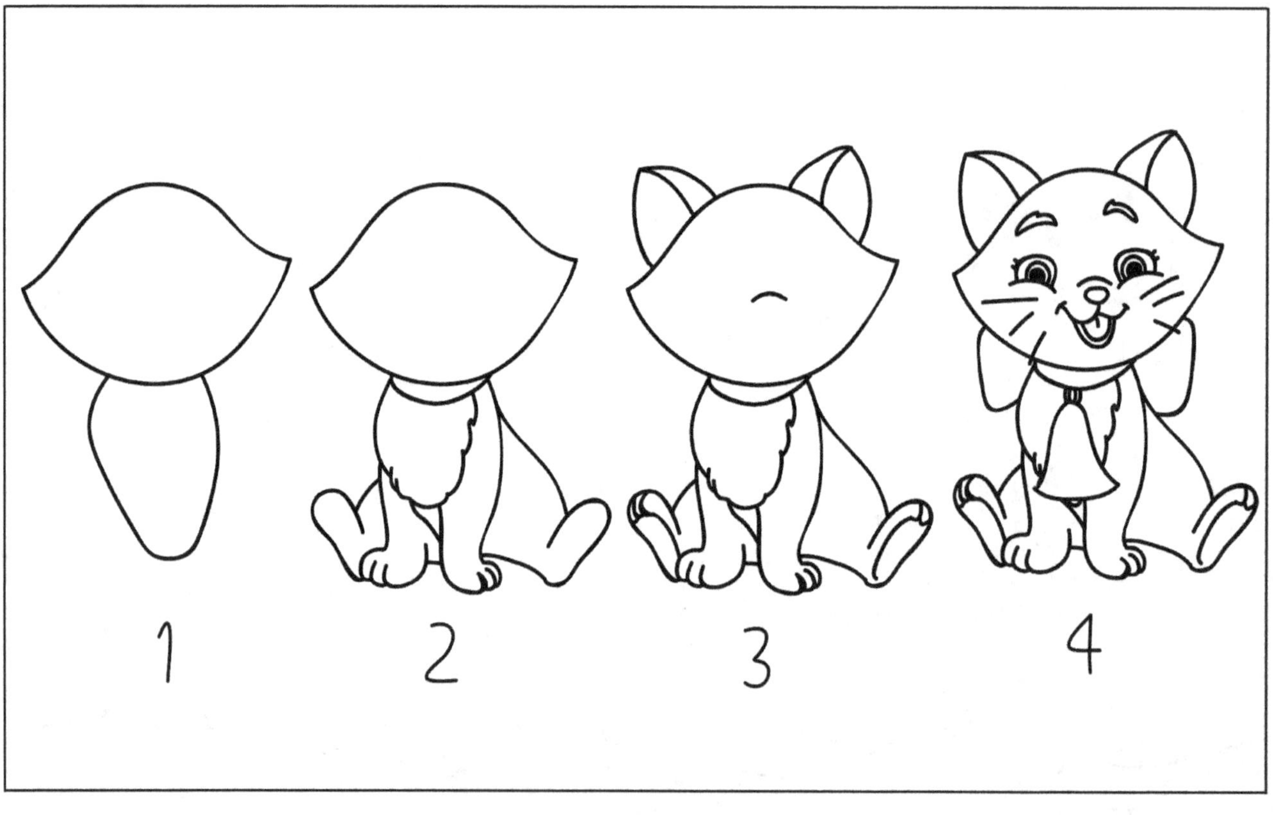

1

2

3

4

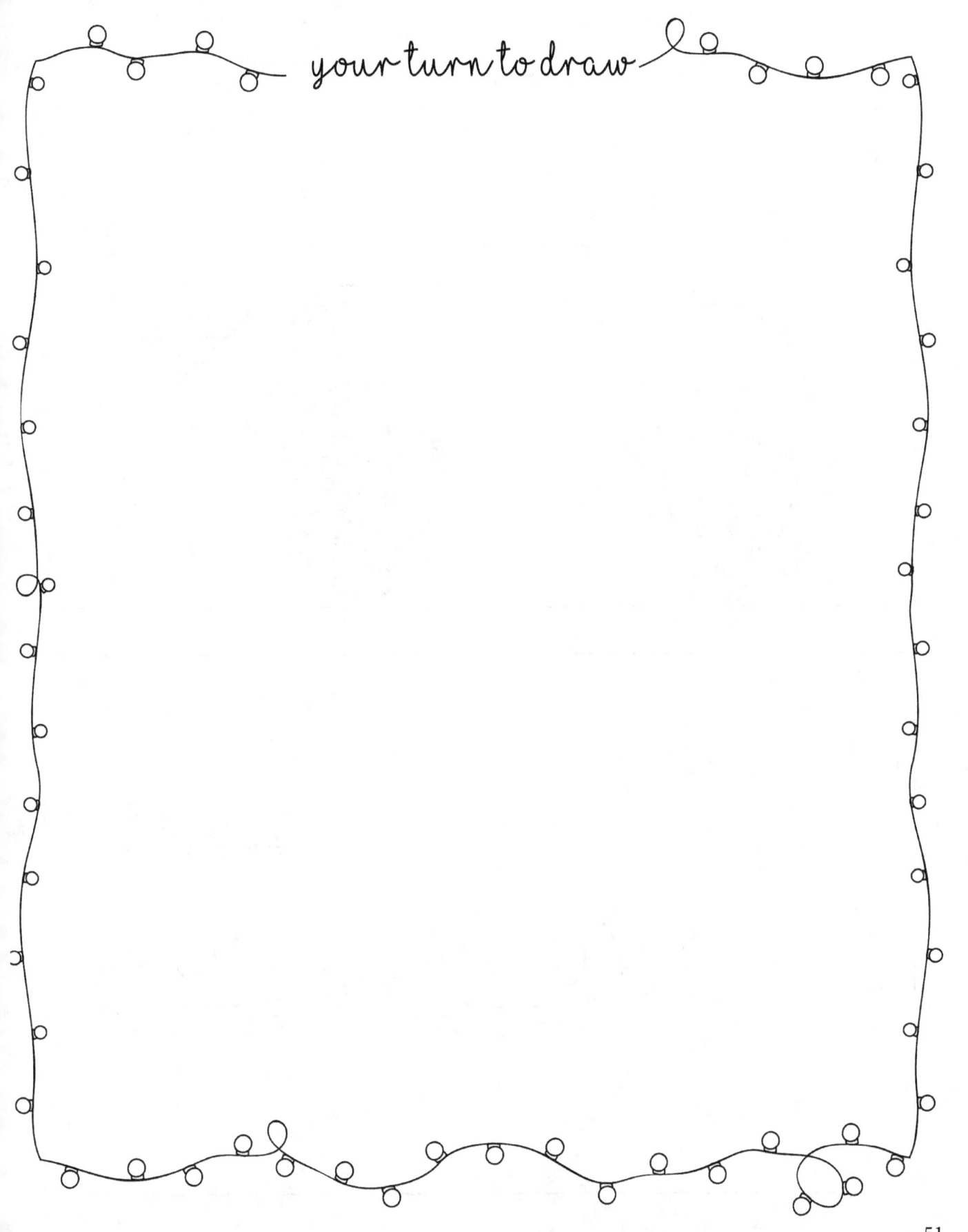

your turn to draw

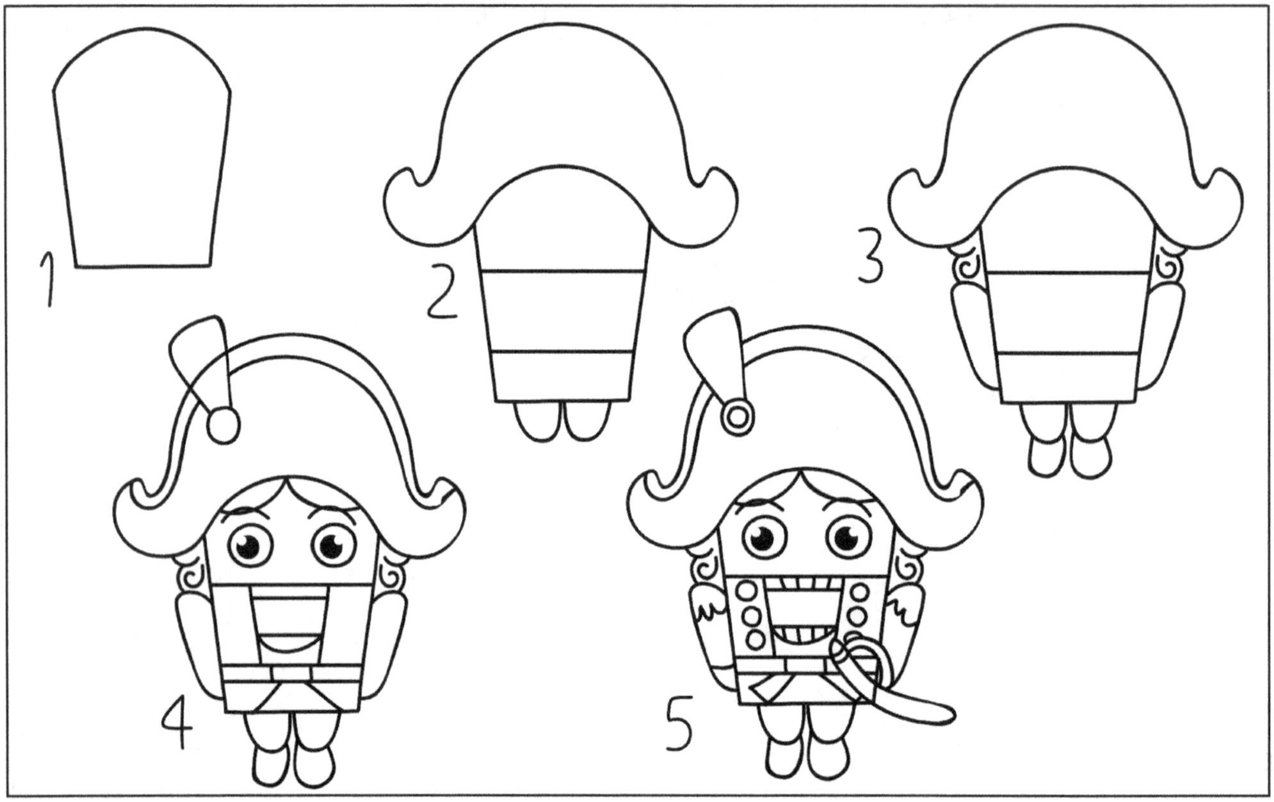

1

2

3

4

5

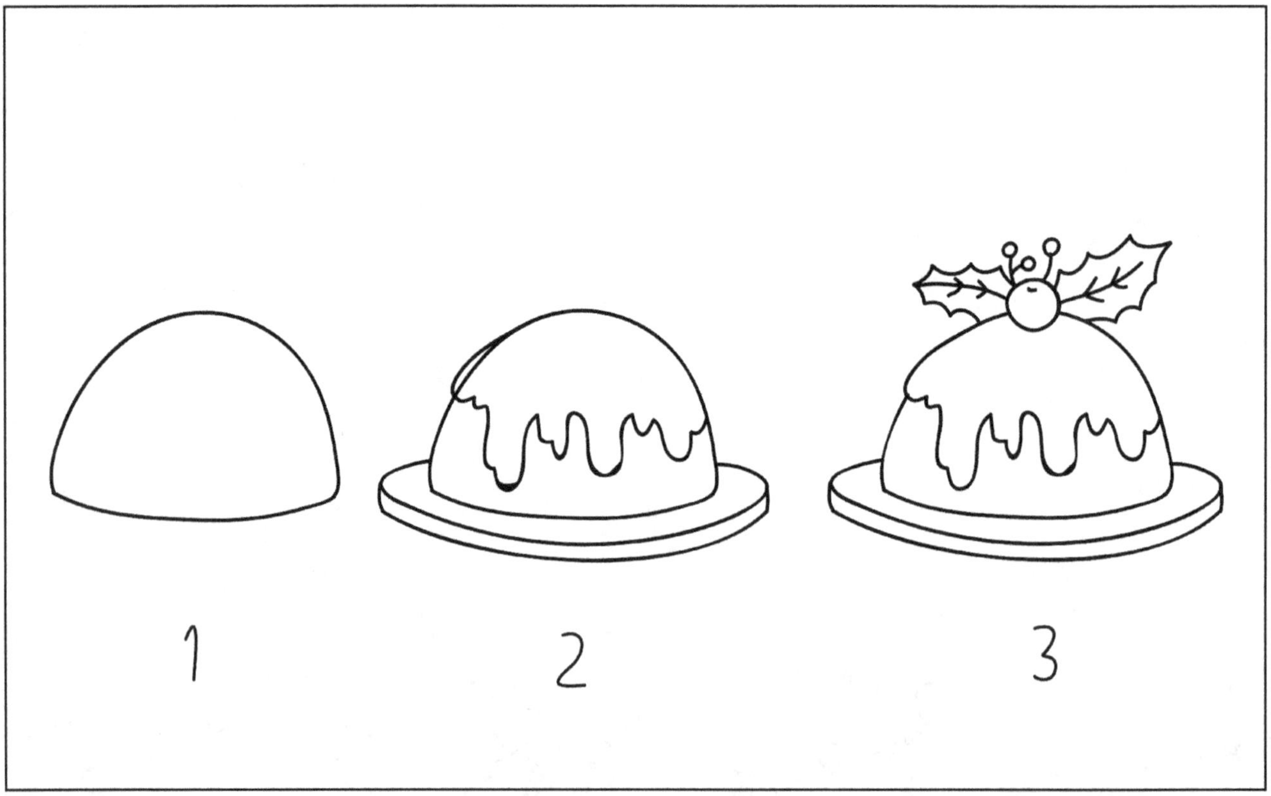

1

2

3

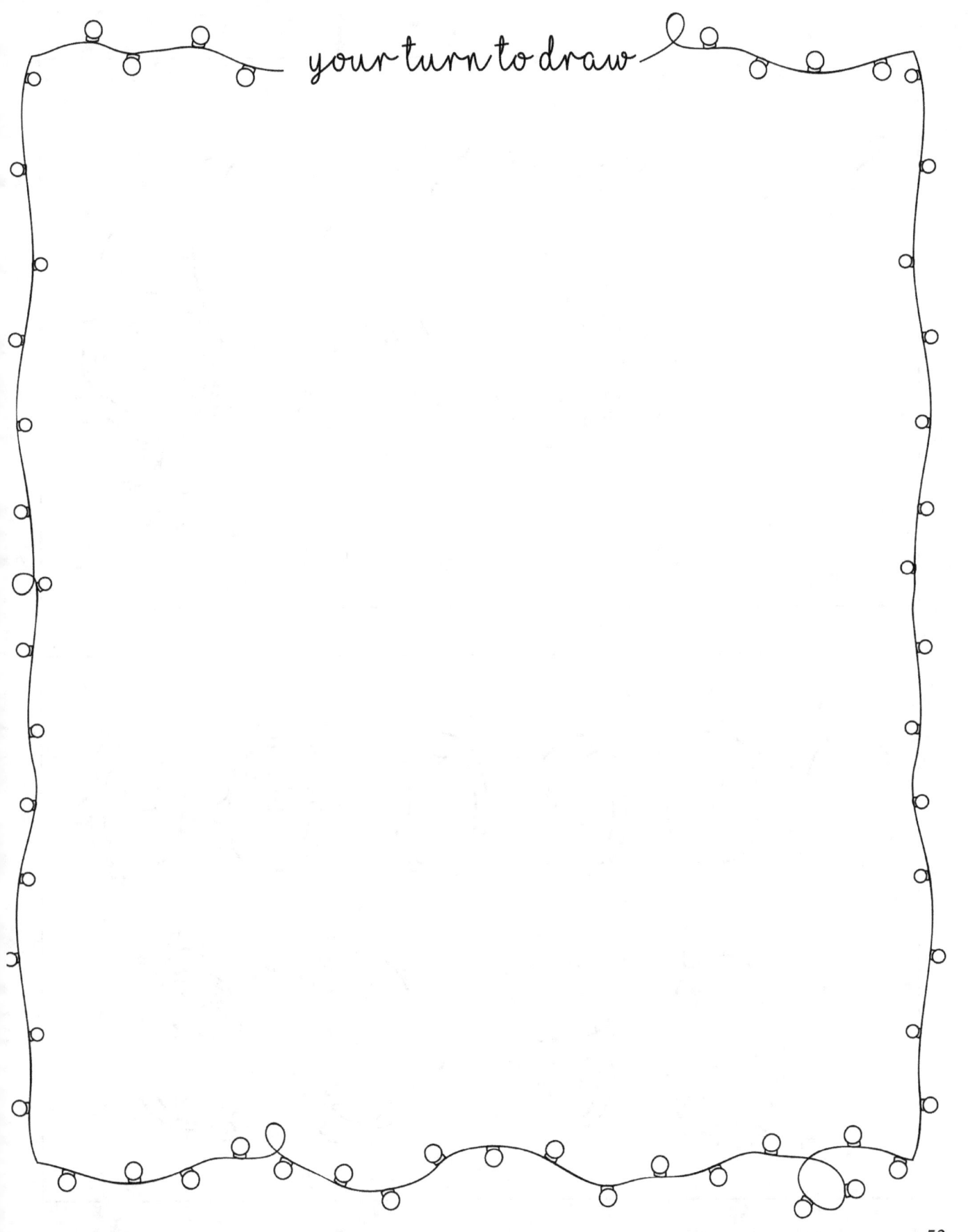

your turn to draw

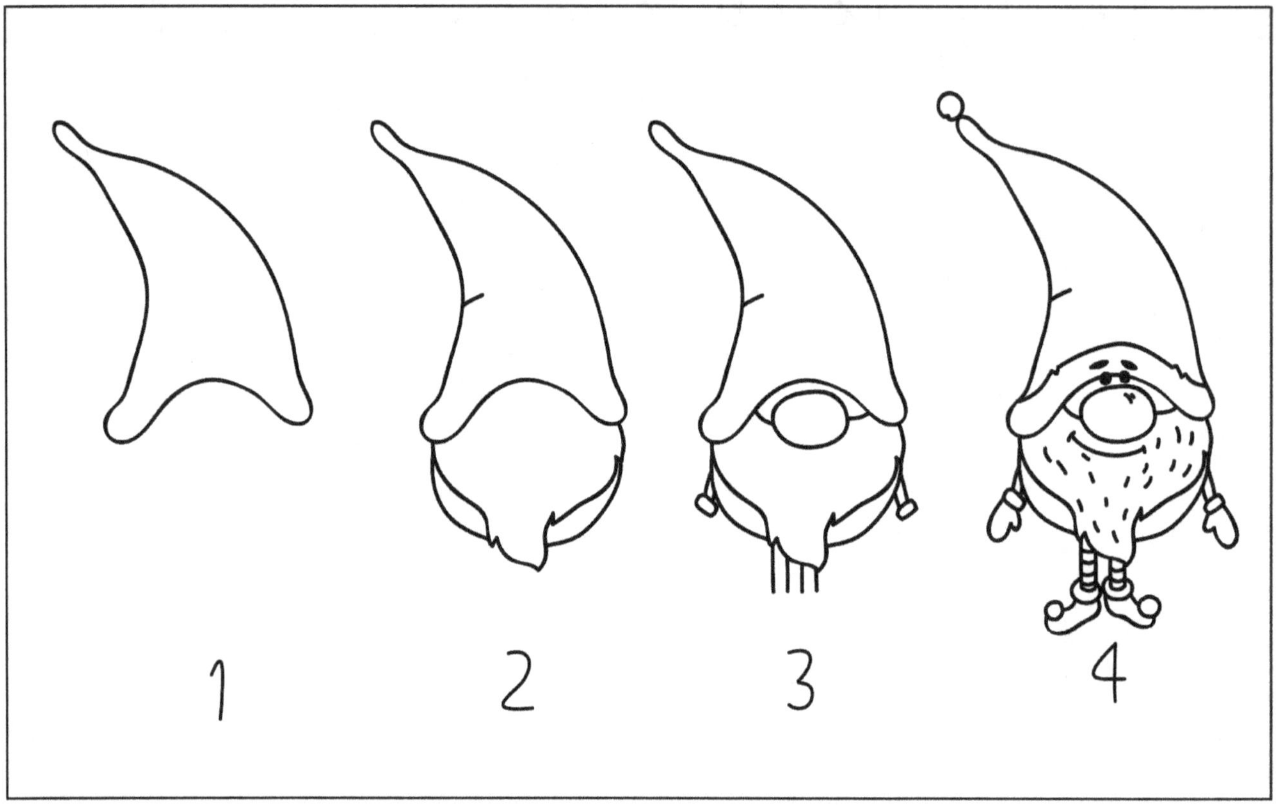

1   2   3   4

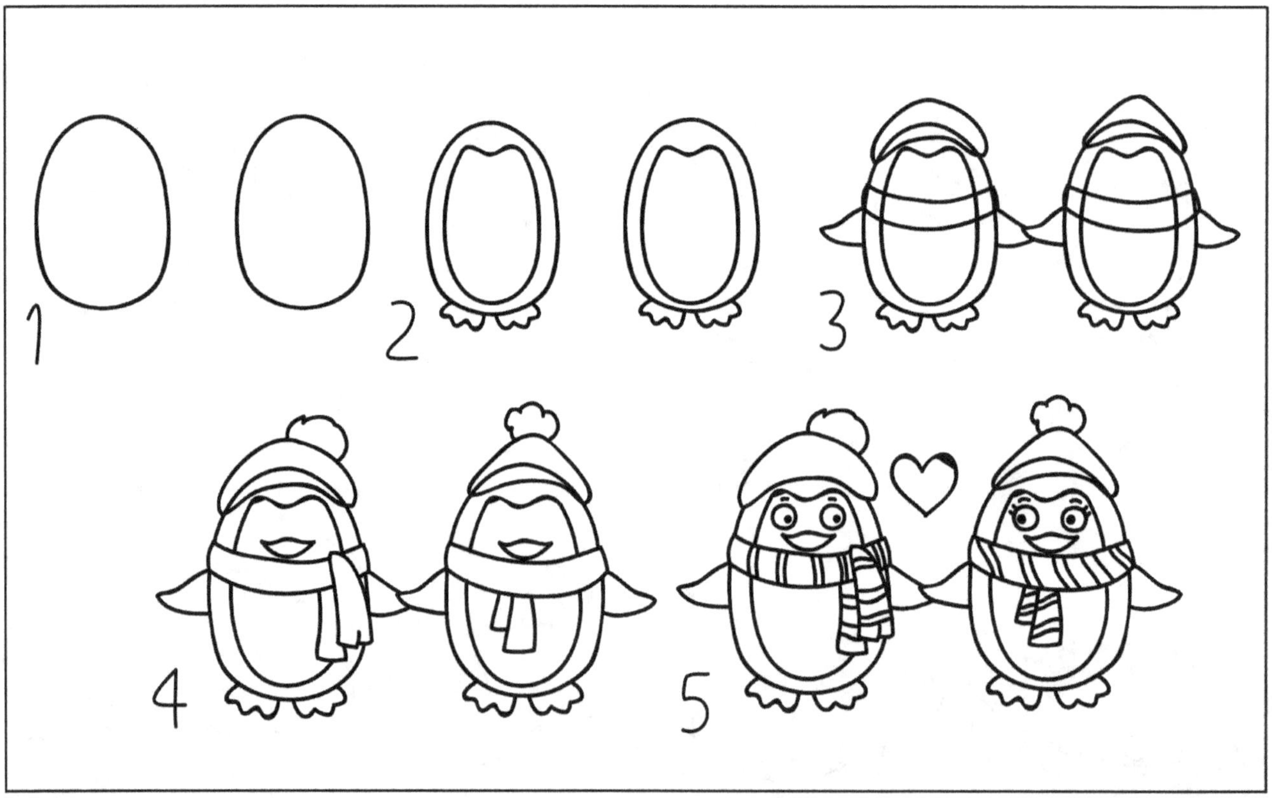

1   2   3   4   5

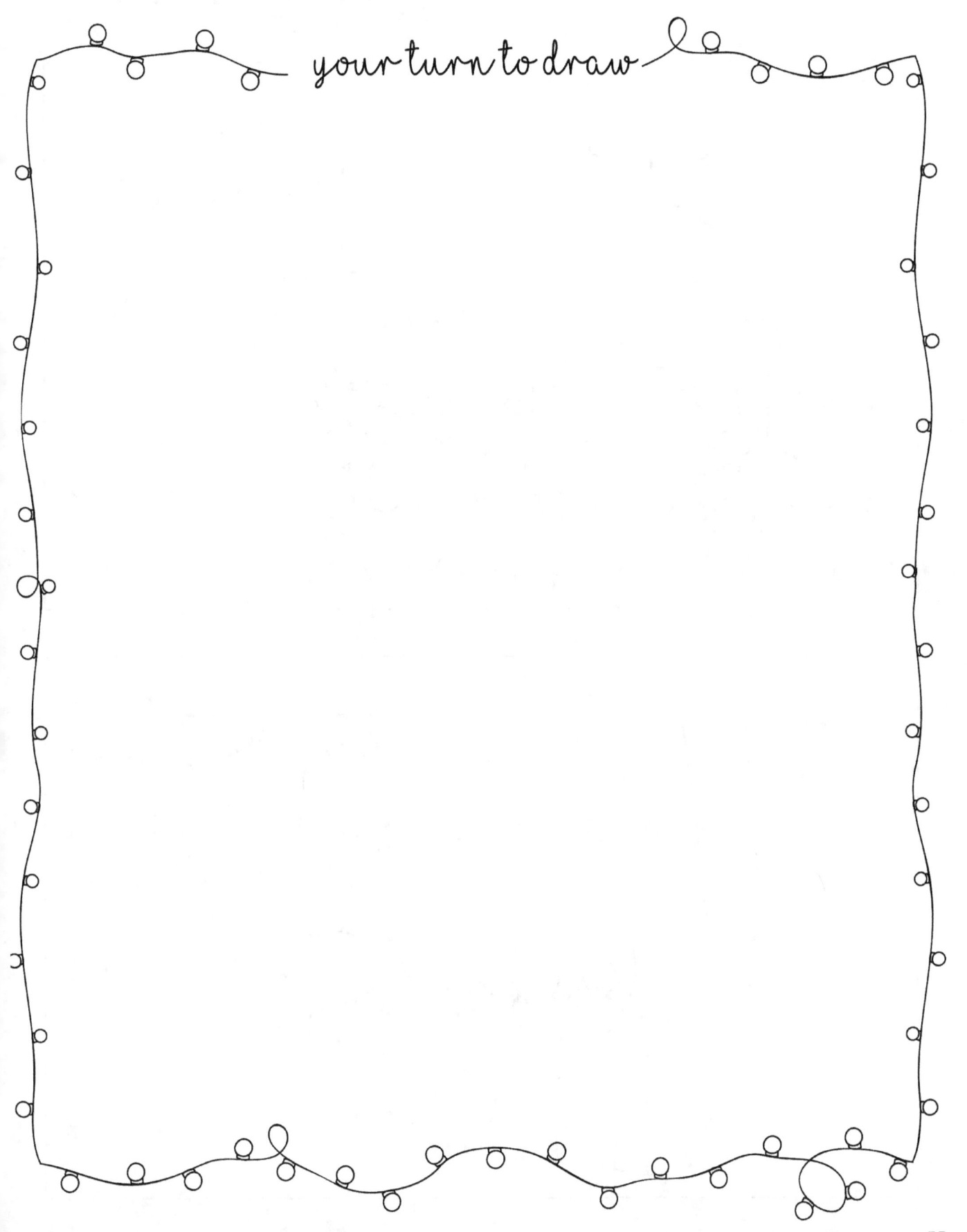

your turn to draw

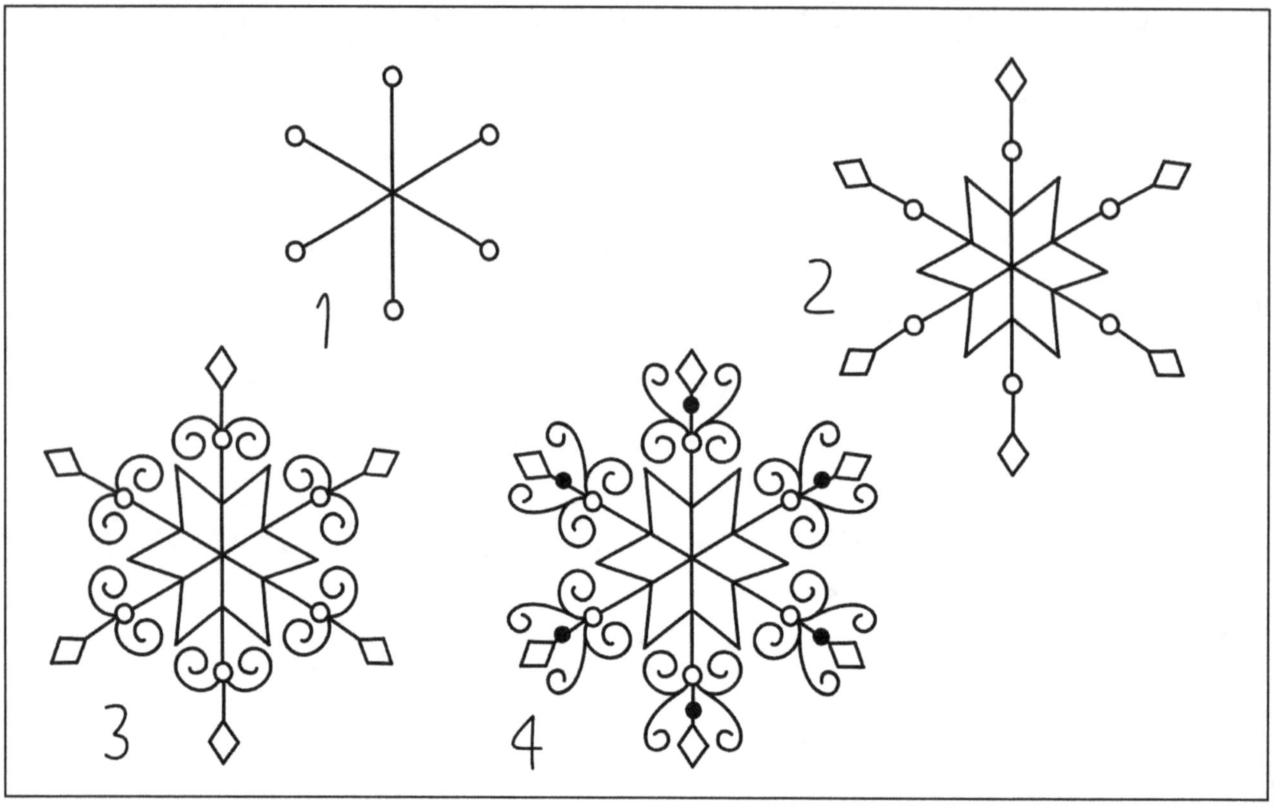

1

2

3

4

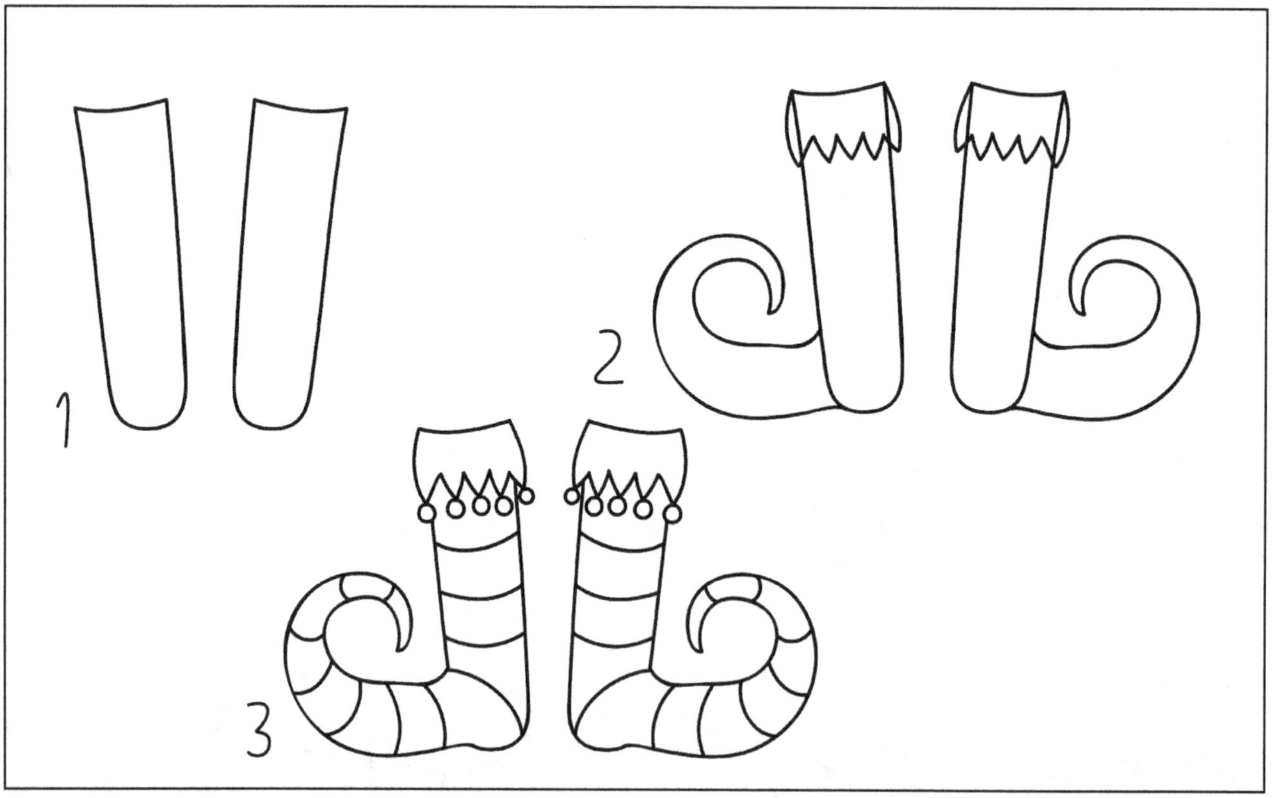

1

2

3

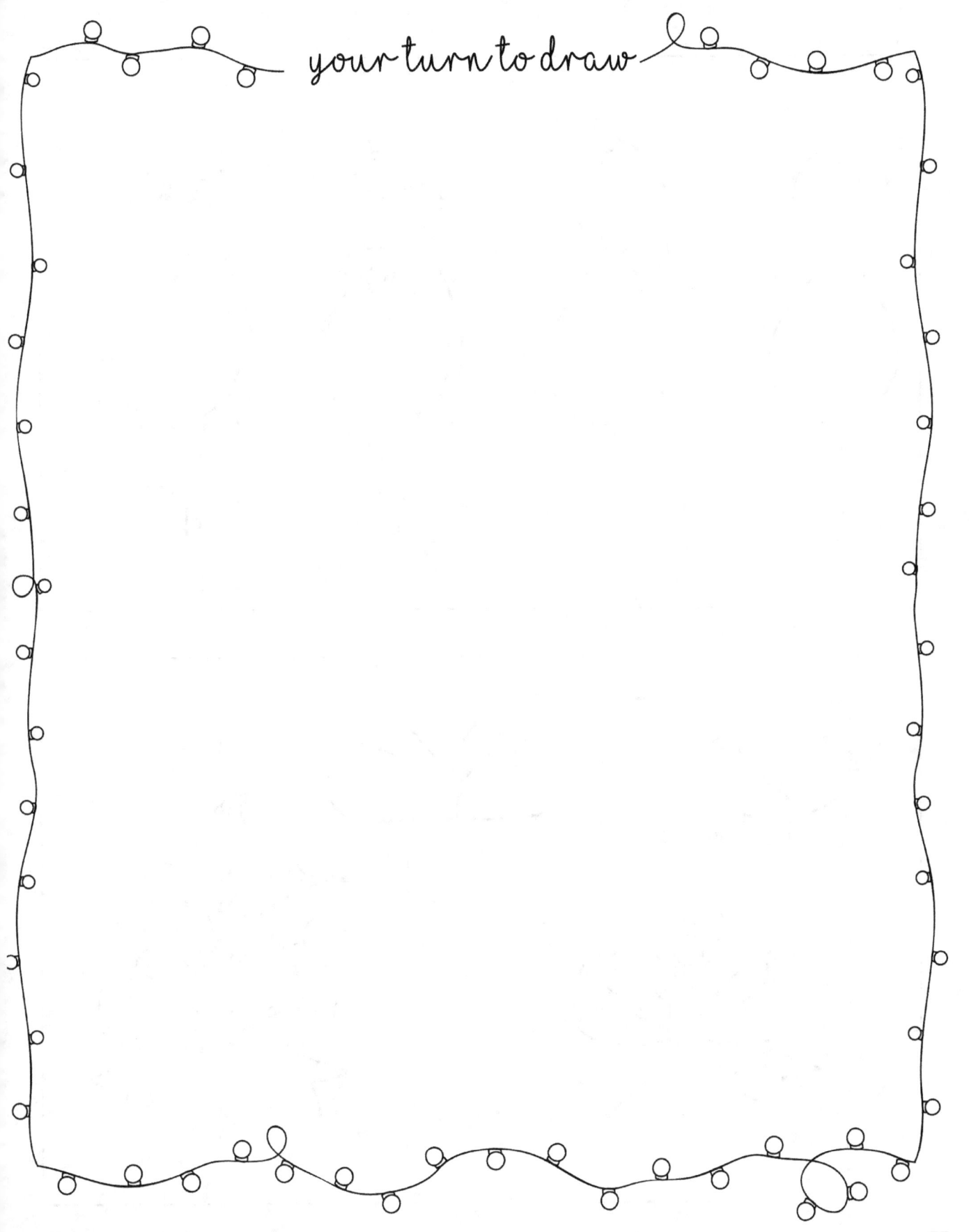

your turn to draw

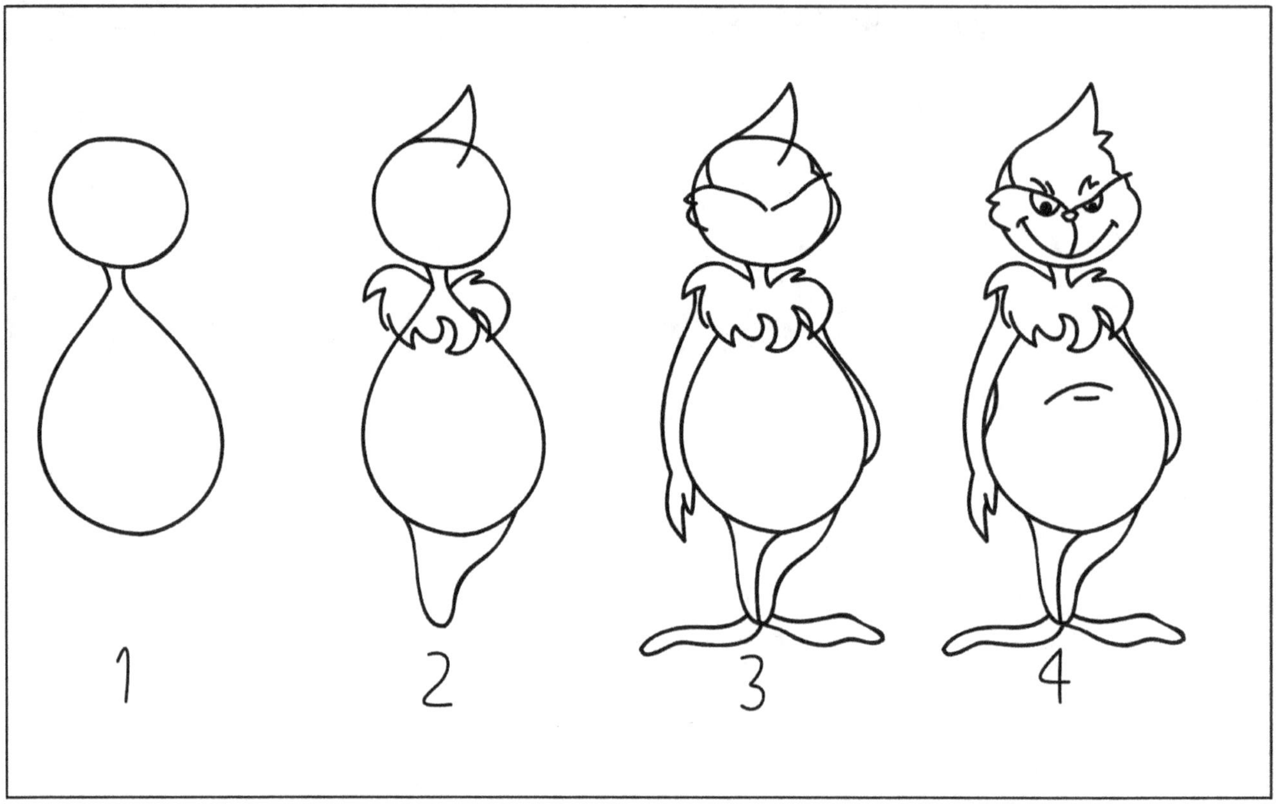

1   2   3   4

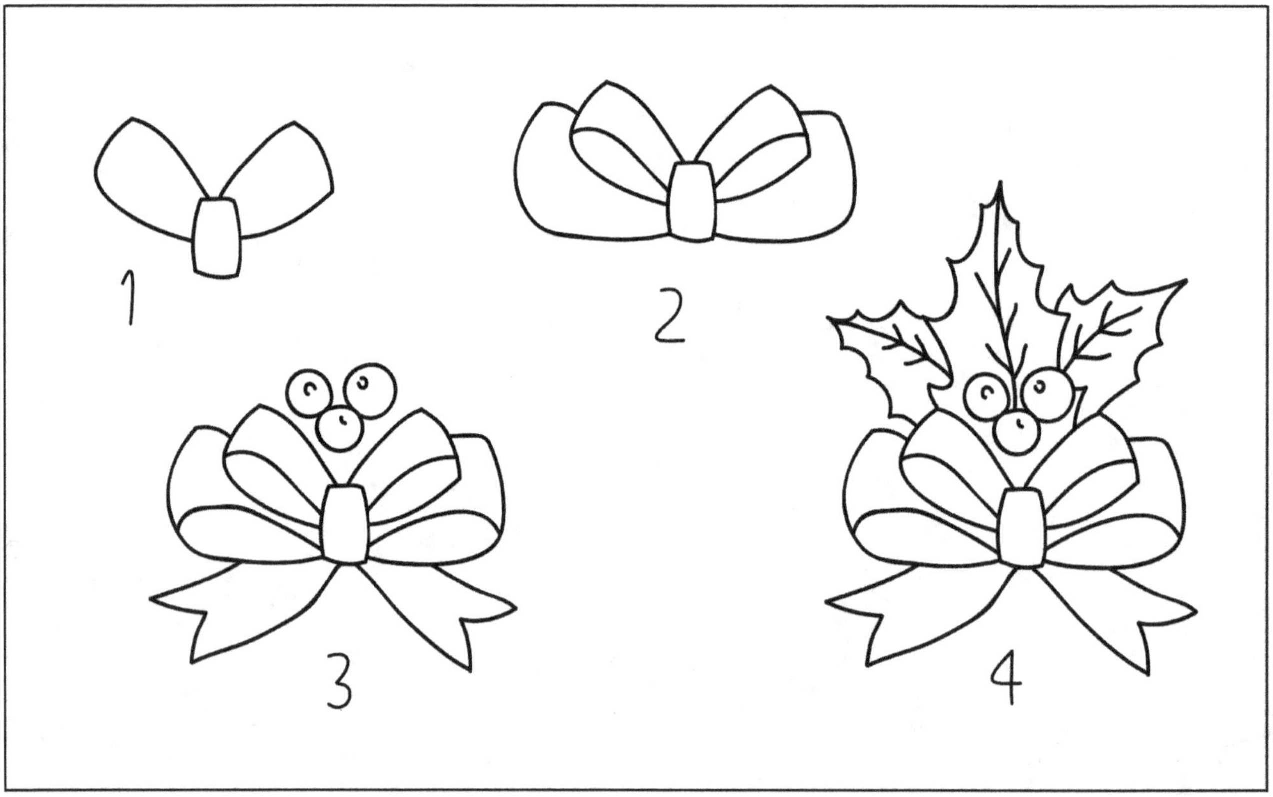

1   2   3   4

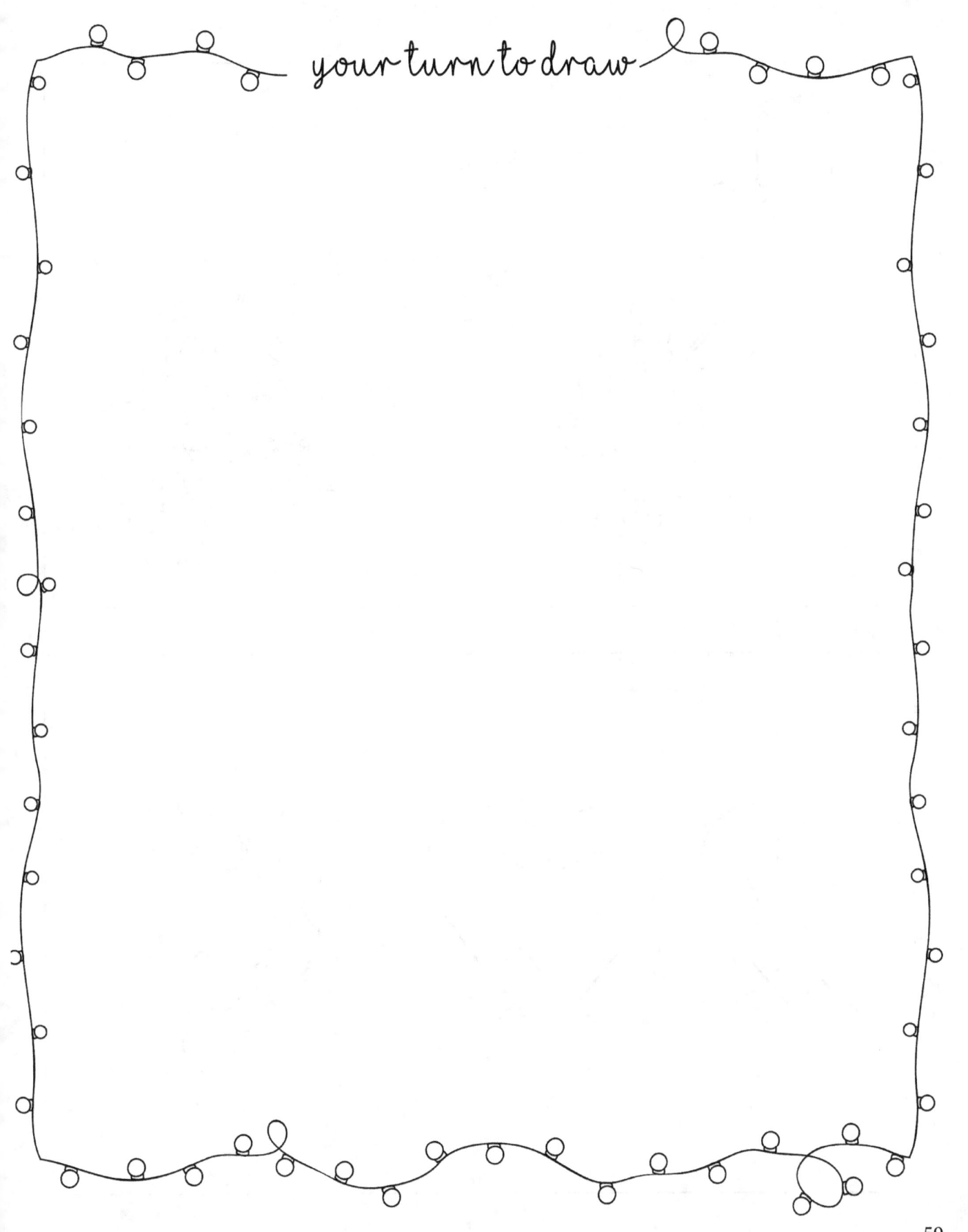

your turn to draw

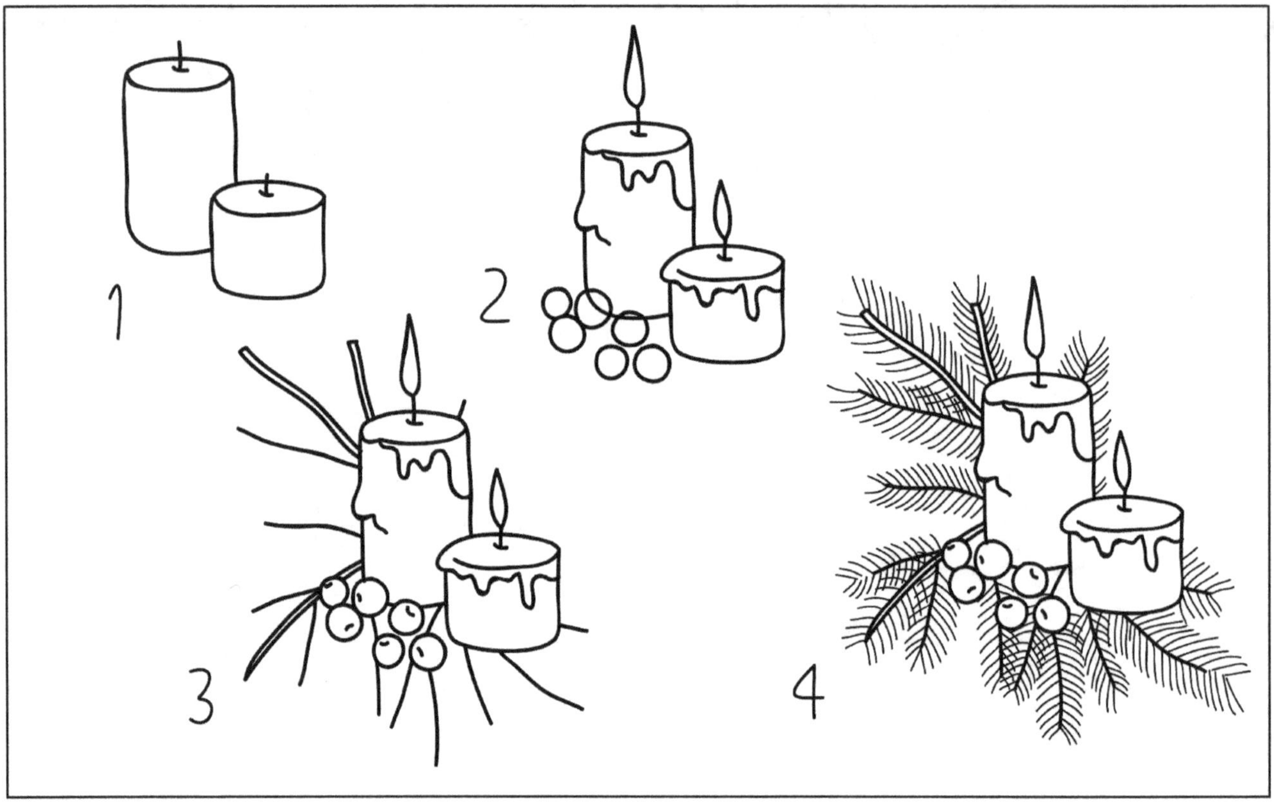

1

2

3

4

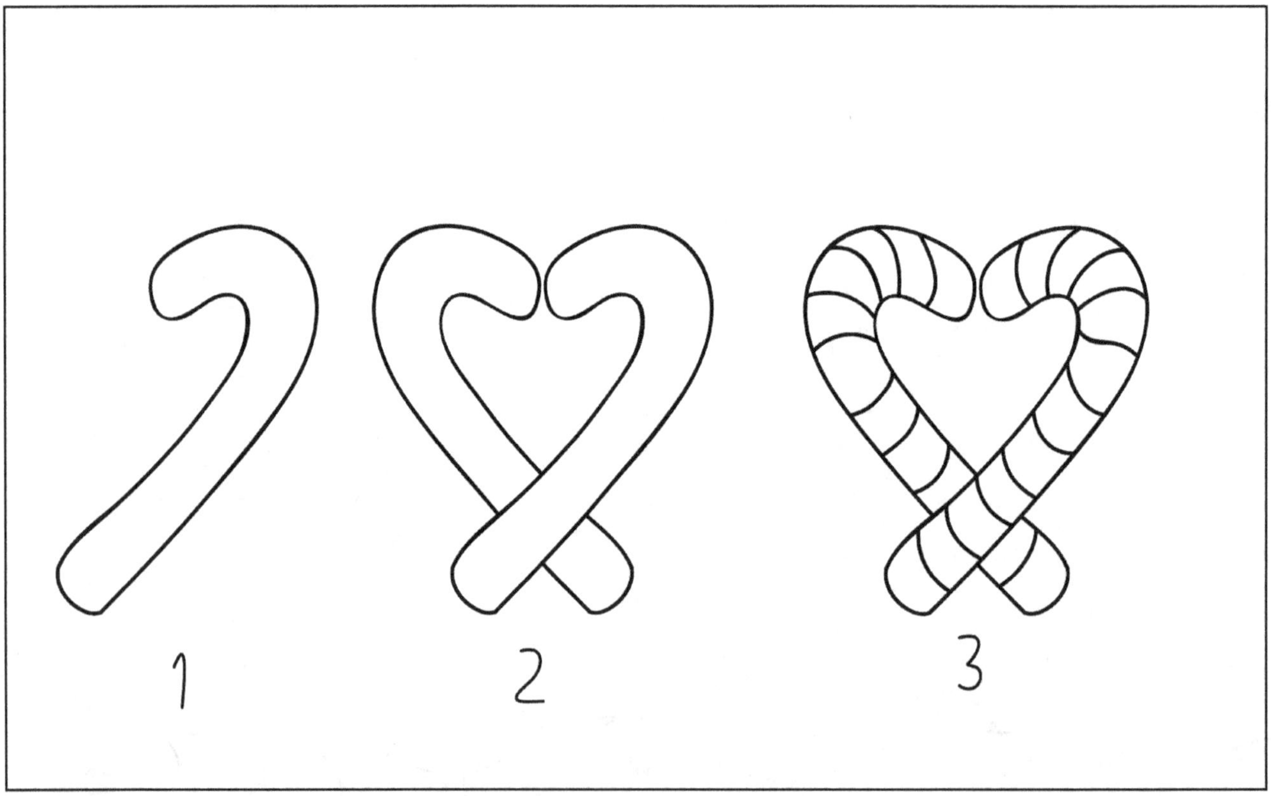

1

2

3

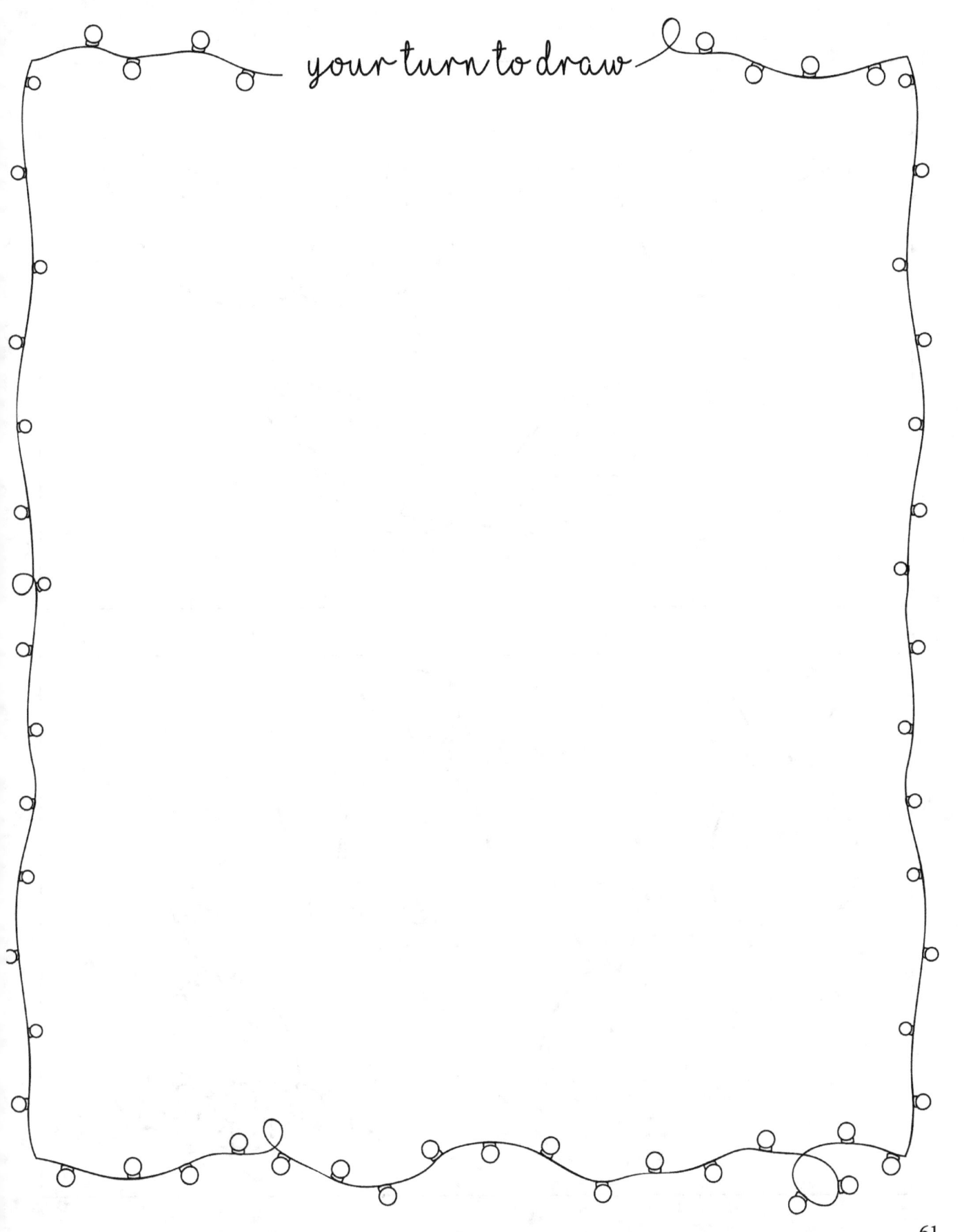

your turn to draw

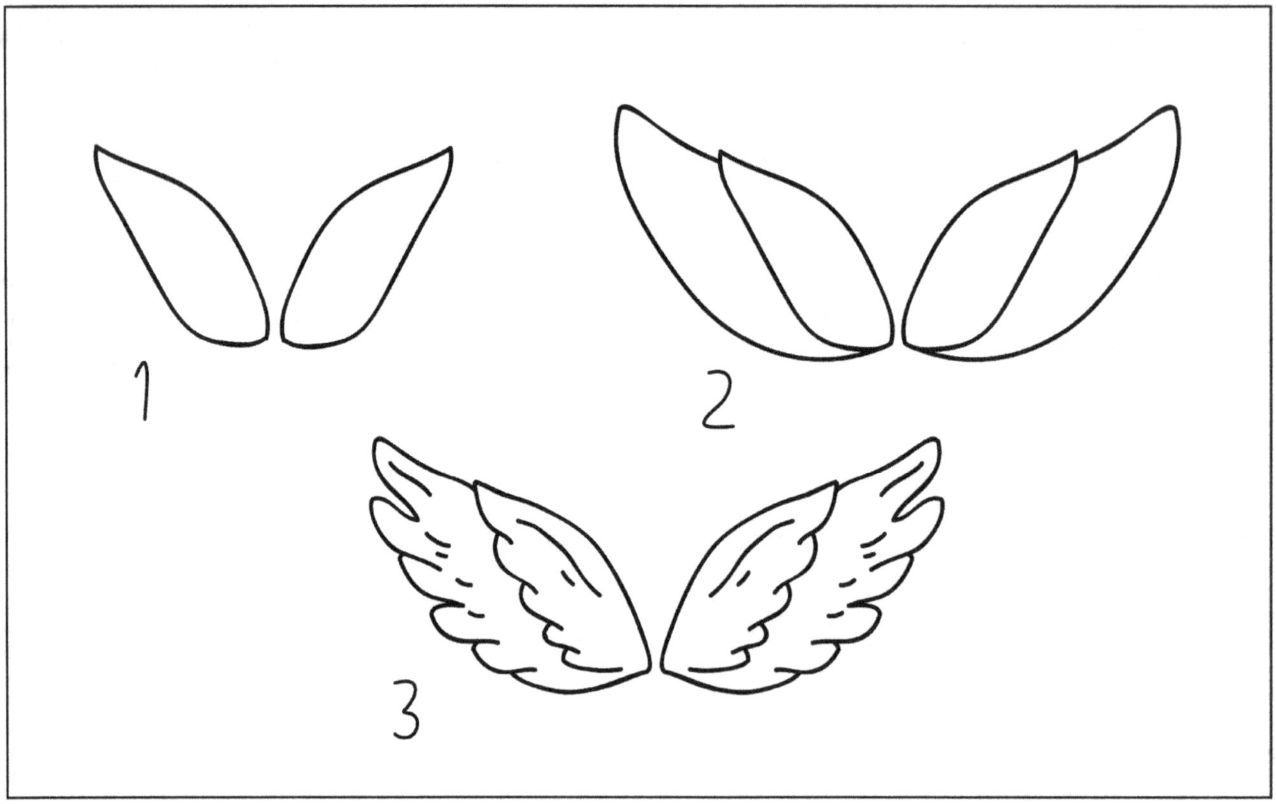

1

2

3

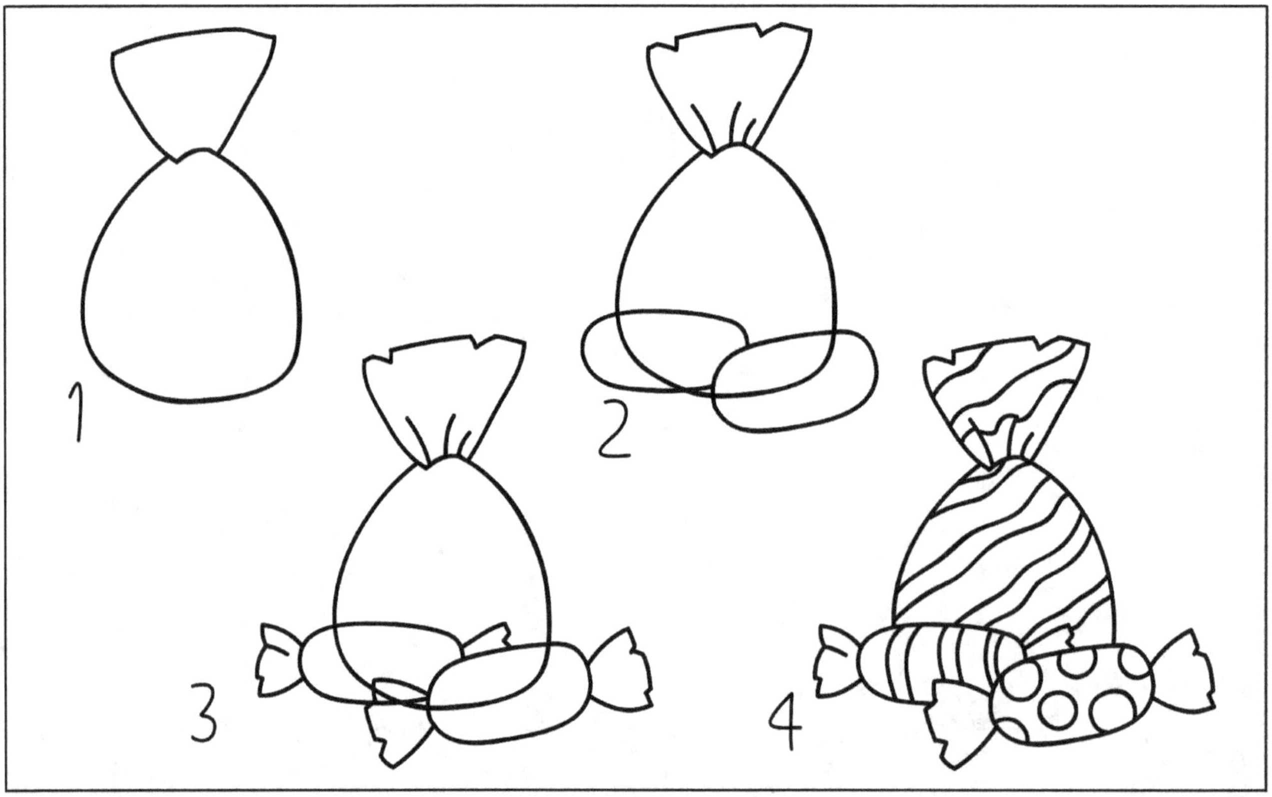

1

2

3

4

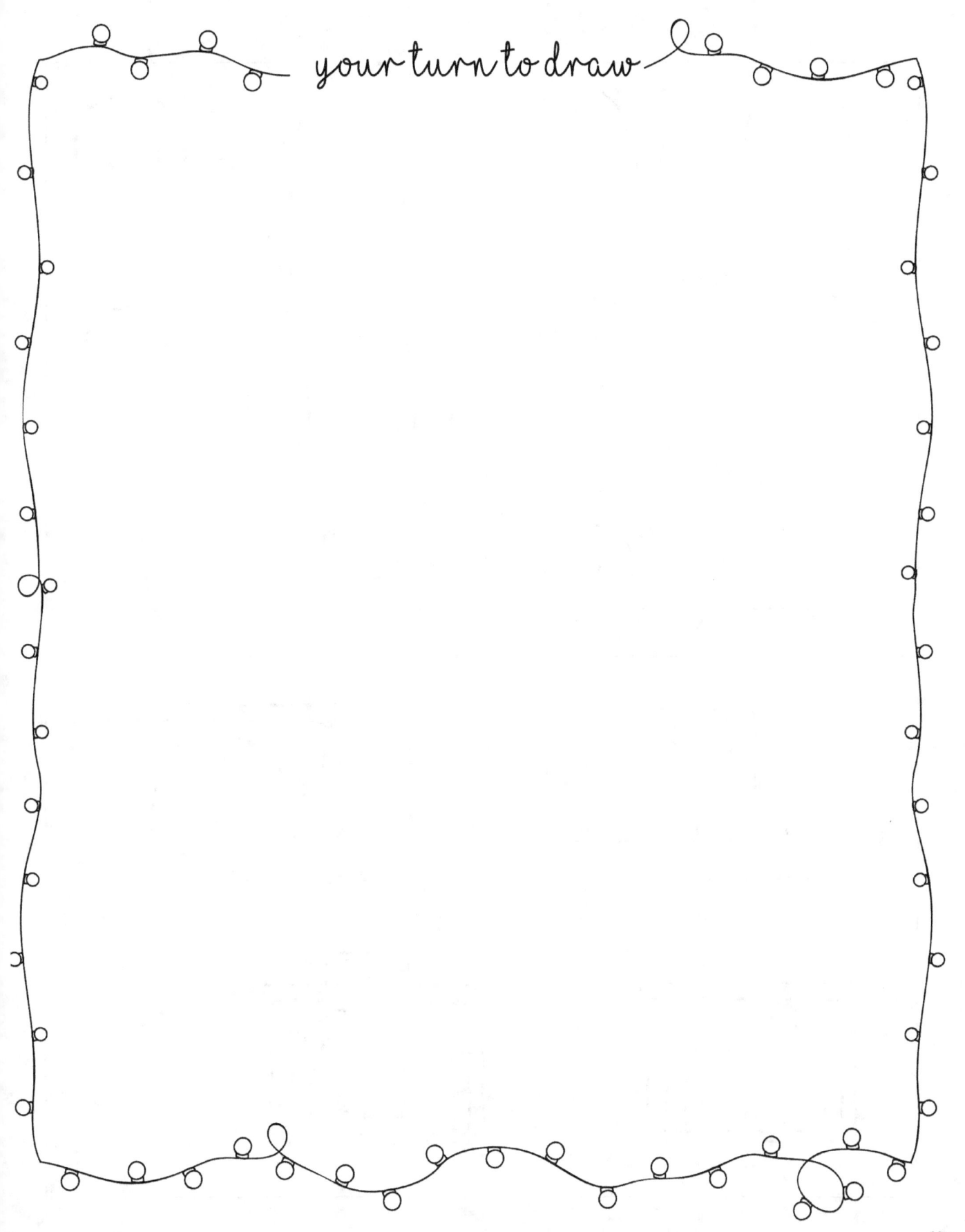

your turn to draw

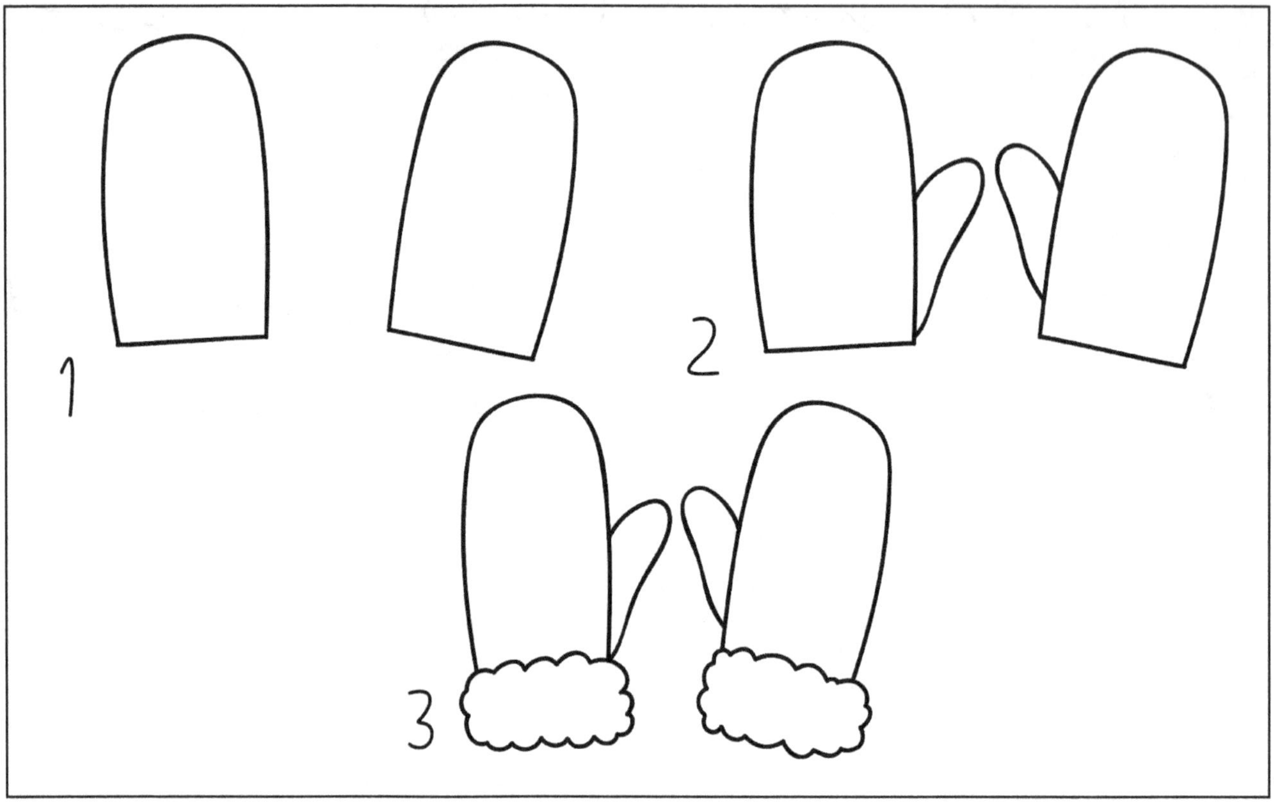

1

2

3

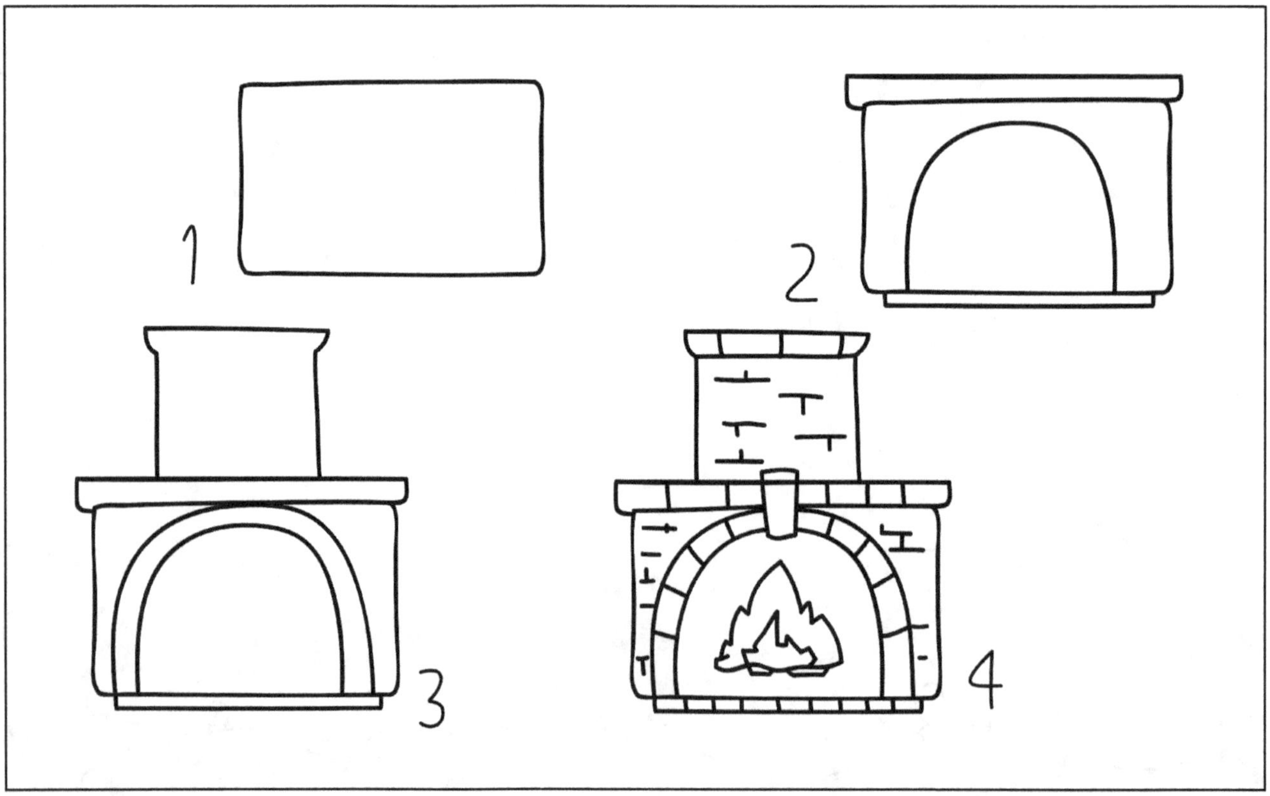

1

2

3

4

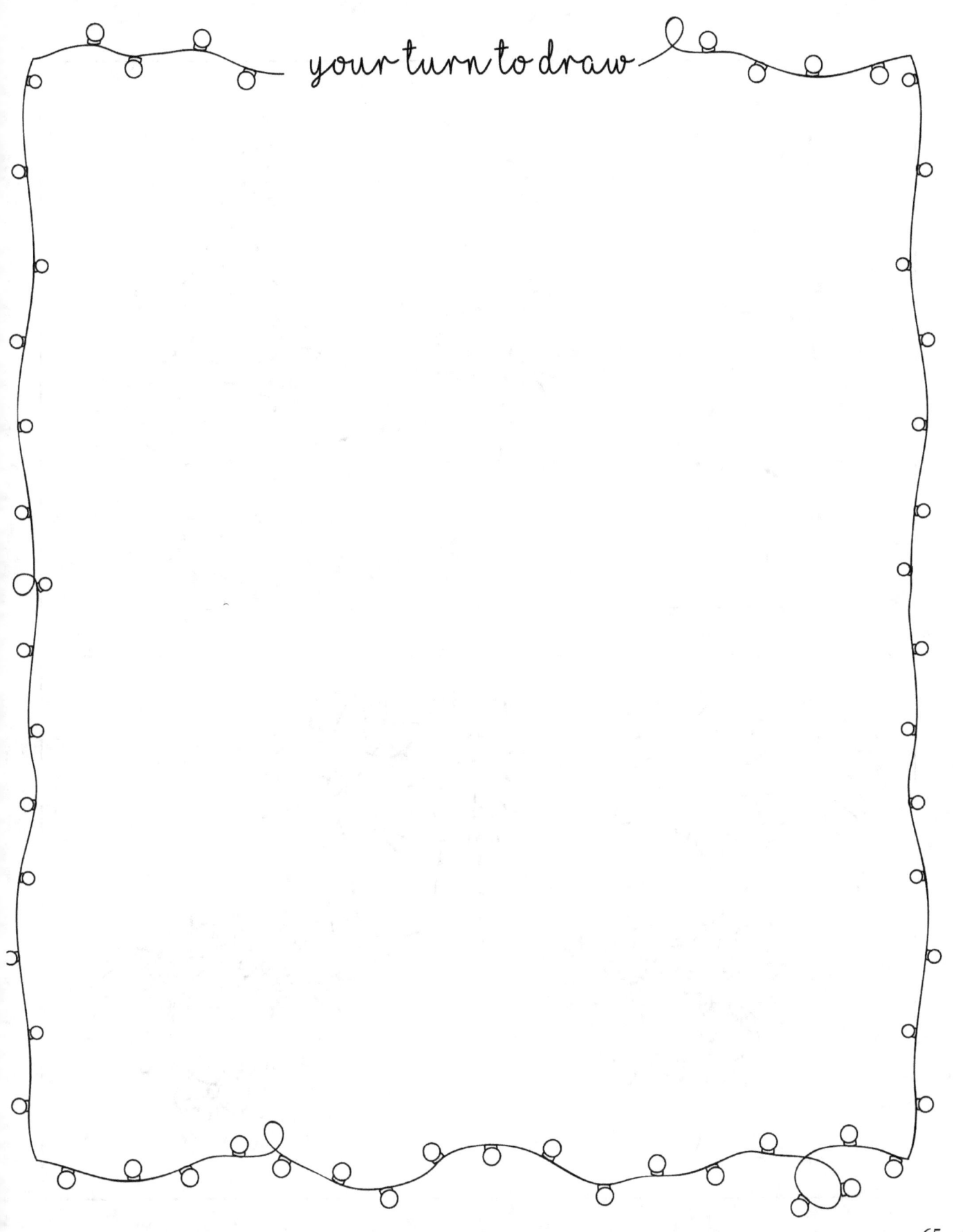

your turn to draw

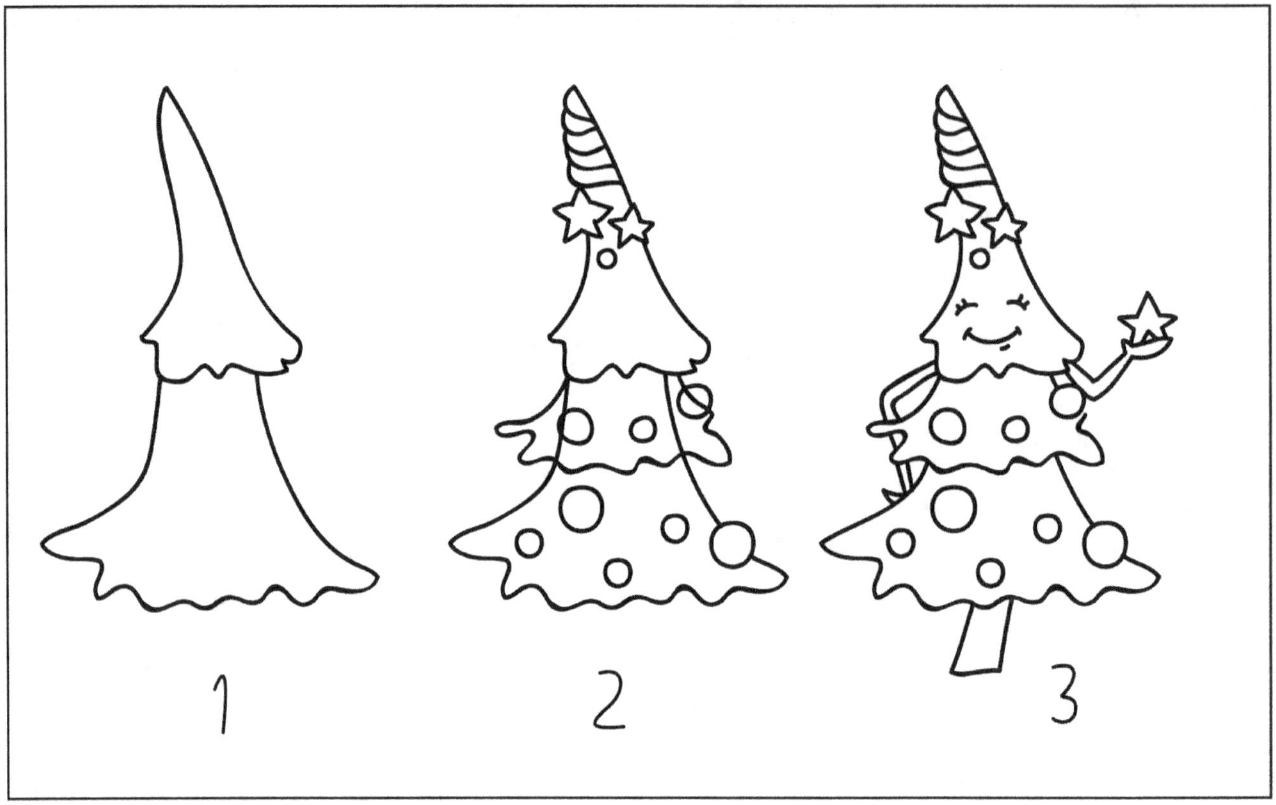

1
2
3

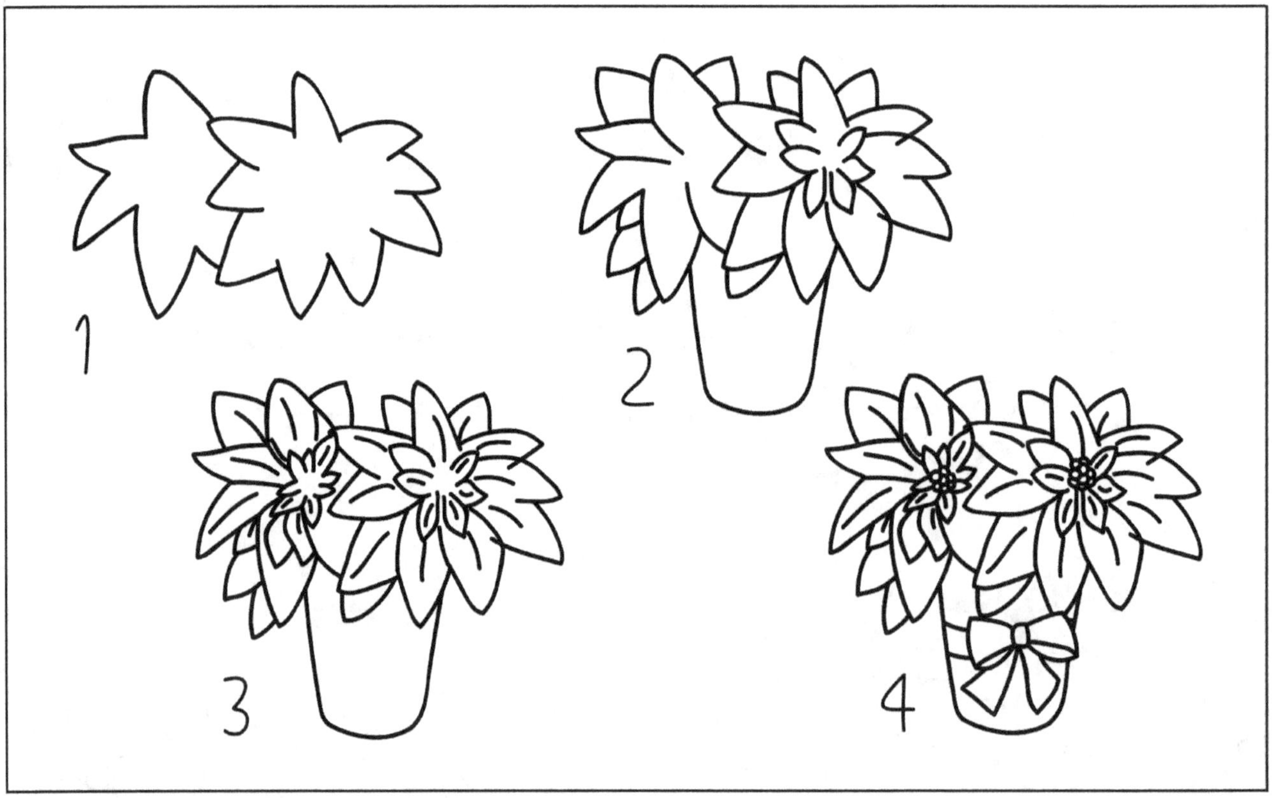

1
2
3
4

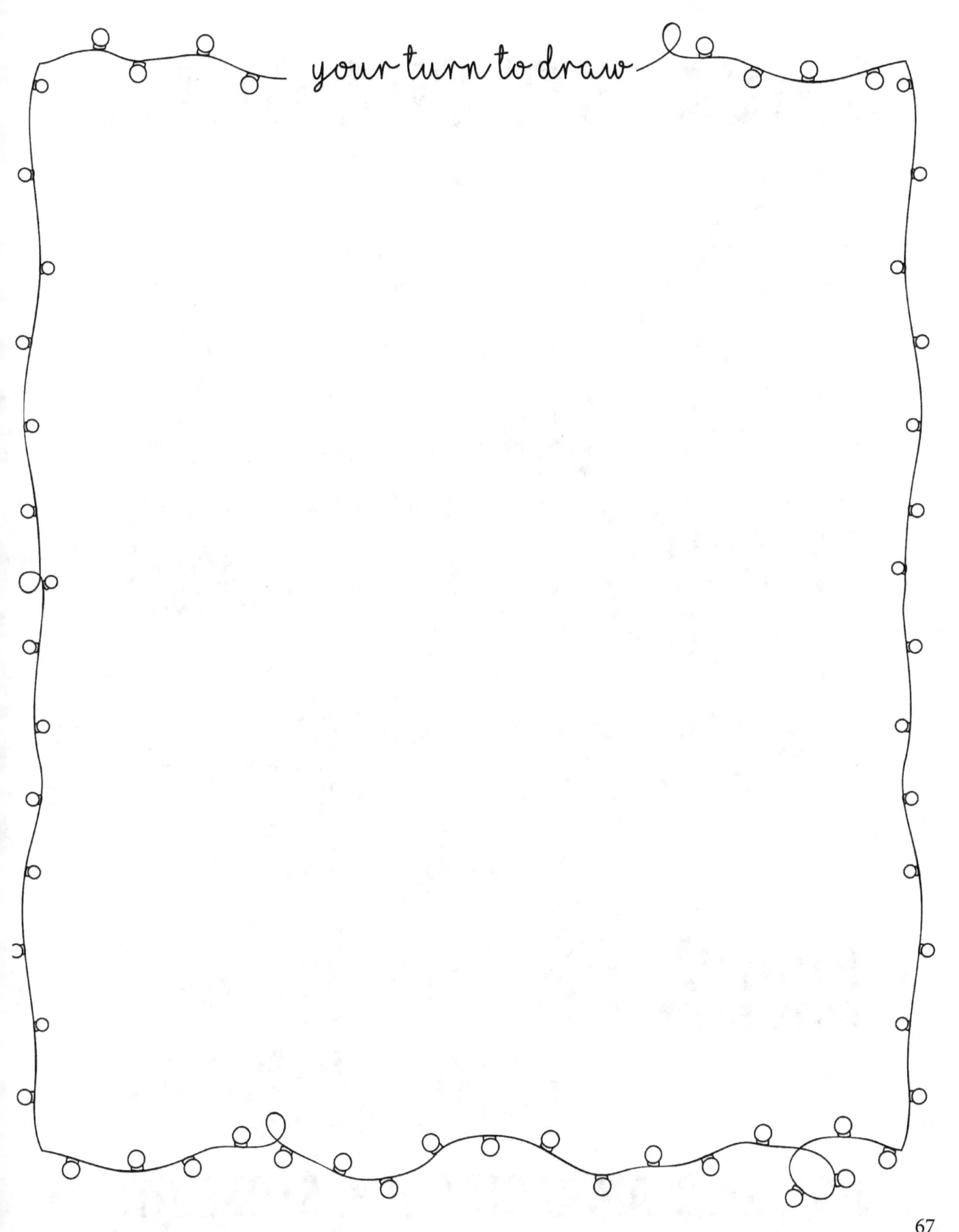

your turn to draw

CHECK OUT OUR OTHER

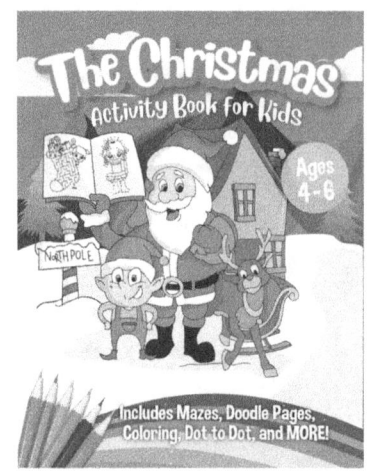

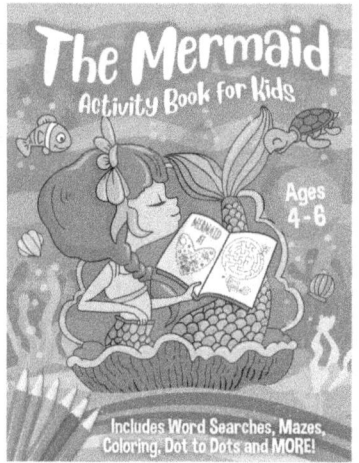

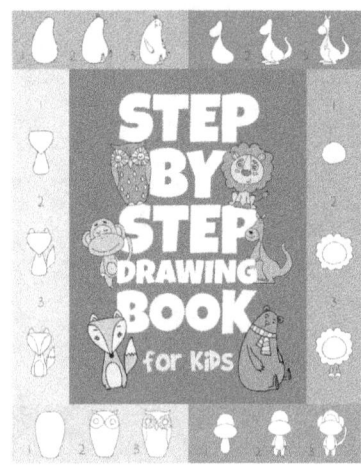

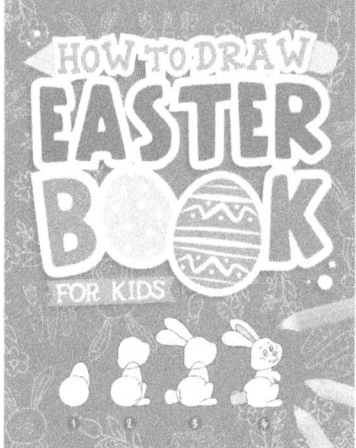

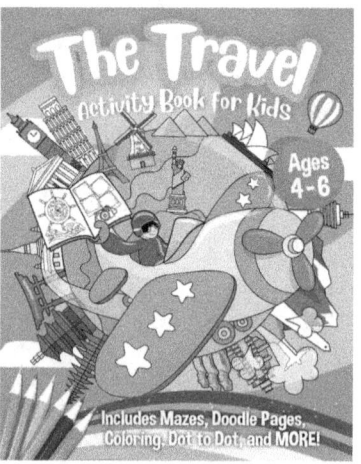

PEANUT PRODIGY

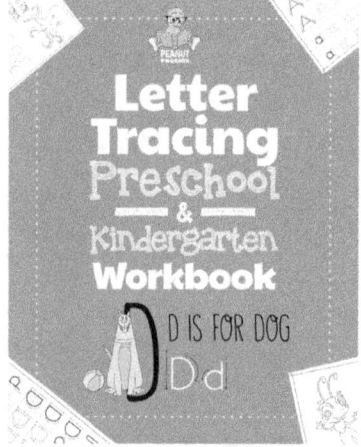

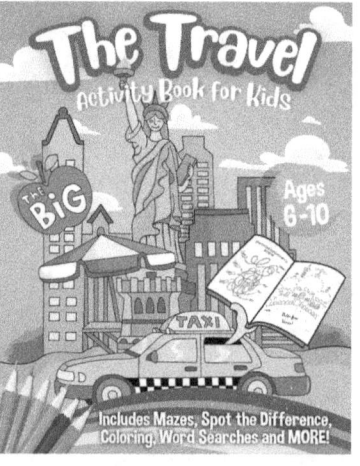

VISIT OUR AMAZON BOOK STORE AT:

PEANUT PRODIGY BOOKS!

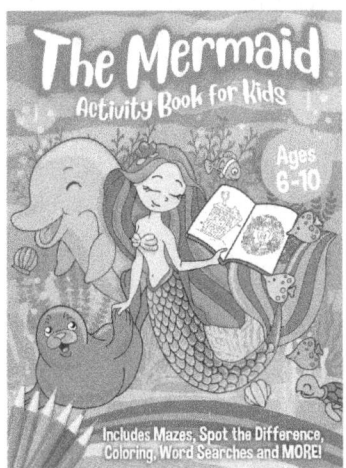
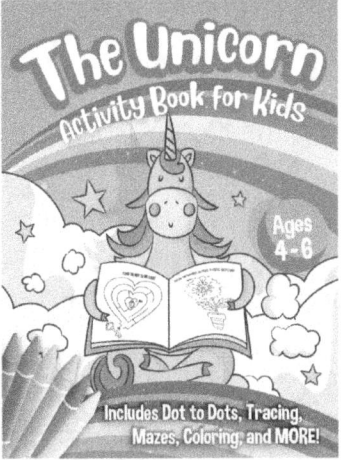
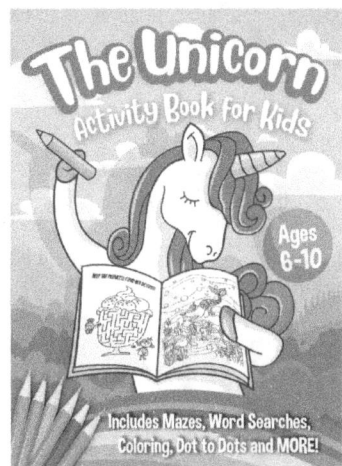
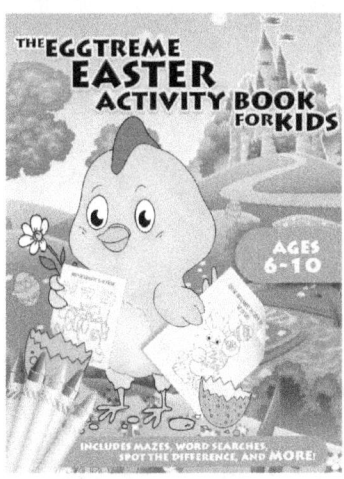
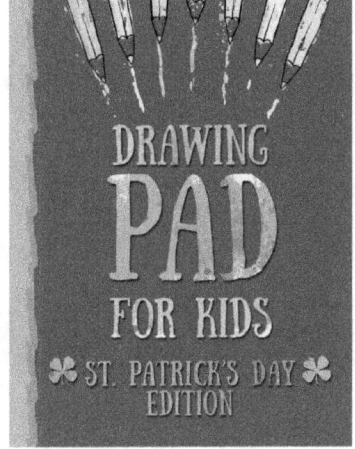
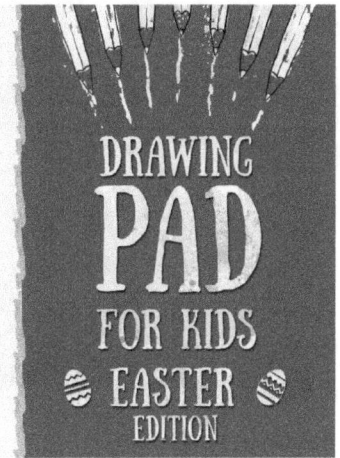
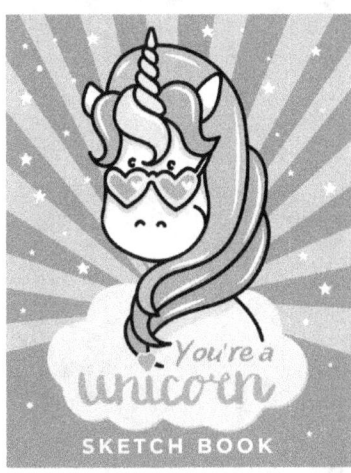
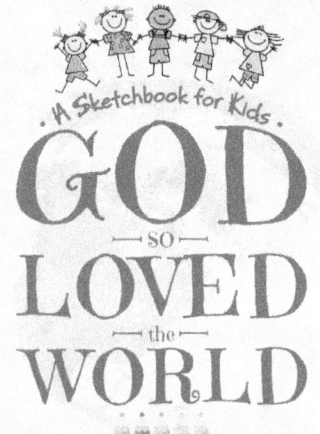
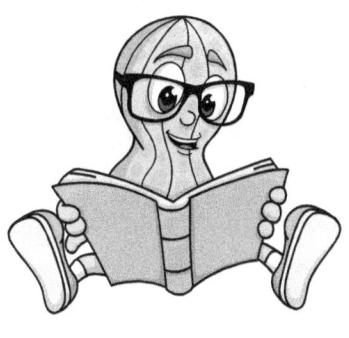